Quick Study

SOCIAL STUDIES

GROWTH OF A NATION

PEARSON

Scott
Foresman

Editorial Offices: Glenview, Illinois • Parsippany, New Jersey • New York, New York
Sales Offices: Parsippany, New Jersey • Duluth, Georgia • Glenview, Illinois •
Coppell, Texas • Ontario, California • Mesa, Arizona

www.sfsocialstudies.com

ISBN 0-328-09007-7

1 2 3 4 5 6 7 8 9 10 V016 12 11 10 09 08 07 06 05 04

Contents

© Scott Foresman Growth of a Nation

Lesson 1: Connections Across Continents

Vocabulary

Ice Age a period of time between 40,000 and 10,000 years ago when the Earth's climate was cold

glaciers thick sheets of ice

migrate to move from one place to another in a group of people

agriculture the knowledge of growing crops and raising animals

cultures the ways of life of a group of people

colony a settlement outside the borders of the country that rules it

Columbian Exchange the trade of people, animals, plants, and ways of life between the Eastern and Western Hemispheres

From Asia to the Americas

The **Ice Age** was a period of time between 40,000 and 10,000 years ago when Earth was very cold. Large amounts of water froze into sheets of ice called **glaciers** and caused ocean levels to drop. Dry land surfaced that used to be under water. A piece of land known as the Bering Strait land bridge connected Asia and North America. People from Asia crossed over it and **migrated,** or moved, throughout North and South America. They hunted large animals such as the woolly mammoth. At the end of the Ice Age, many large animals died out. People hunted smaller animals, fished, and gathered plants. About 7,000 years ago, in the area now known as Mexico, people learned how to grow crops and raise animals. Farming, or **agriculture,** made it possible for people to live in one place.

Native American Cultures

By the 1400s, people had developed different ways of life, or **cultures,** throughout the land that is now the United States. In the Eastern Woodlands region, Native American groups such as the Iroquois hunted forest animals. Iroquois families lived together in wooden buildings called longhouses. On the Great Plains, the Lakota and Pawnee hunted herds of buffalo. While on the hunt, groups lived in tepees made

of poles and buffalo hides. In the Southwest, the Hopi and Zuni groups lived in villages. They farmed the dry land by creating ditches that carried stream water to crops. In the Northwest Coast region, the Kwakiutl and Tlingit fished, hunted, and gathered plants for their food.

East Meets West

In the 1200s and 1300s, trade increased among people in Asia, Africa, and Europe. In Europe, better designed ships and inventions like the Chinese-made compass allowed explorers to go far distances. One explorer, Christopher Columbus, sought a new trade route by sailing west from Spain to Asia. Instead, he landed on the Bahama Islands in North America in 1492. European countries began to establish **colonies** in North and South America. Farm animals such as horses and cattle were brought to the Americas. Native American foods such as corn and potatoes were sent to Europe. This trade between the Eastern and Western Hemispheres was called the **Columbian Exchange.** Europeans also brought smallpox and measles. Many Native Americans died, since they had no defense against the new diseases. As the colonies grew, Native American people were also forced off their land or enslaved.

Lesson 1: Review

1. 🔄 **Summarize** Fill in two details that support the summary below.

> The first Americans hunted mammoths.

> Life in North America changed in many ways from the Ice Age to the arrival of the Europeans.

2. How did Ice Age glaciers allow people to migrate from Asia to the Americas?

_____

_____

_____

3. How did Native Americans of the different cultural regions get their food?

_____

_____

_____

4. How did life for Native Americans change after Columbus's voyage to the Americas?

_____

_____

_____

5. **Critical Thinking:** *Interpret Charts* Based on the flow chart on page 10 of your textbook, do you think Europe benefited from the Columbian Exchange? Explain your answer.

_____

_____

_____

_____

Lesson 2: Life in the Colonies

Vocabulary

cash crop a crop grown to sell for profit

House of Burgesses the first law-making assembly in the English colonies

economy a system for producing and distributing goods and services

natural resource a useful material found in nature

plantations large farms that grew cash crops and housed workers

triangular trade routes trade routes for slaves and goods that formed a triangle between Africa, the colonies, and Europe

French and Indian War a war in which the British defeated the French and their American Indian allies in North America

Founding Colonies

Colonies were established in North America by the 1600s. Many became centers of trade. French settlers founded Quebec in 1608. It became a center for beaver fur trade. Dutch settlers founded New Amsterdam in 1624 on the island of Manhattan. Settlers came to make money from trade and new industries, and in search of land and religious freedom.

First Permanent English Colony

English settlers founded Jamestown, Virginia in 1607. The Powhatan Indians provided corn that helped them survive. In 1612 John Rolfe began growing tobacco to sell it in England. The **cash crop** brought money to Virginia. He also married a Powhatan woman, Pocahontas. In 1619 Virginians created the **House of Burgesses.**

Religious Freedom

English Pilgrims and Puritans came seeking religious freedom. In 1620 Pilgrims on board the *Mayflower* landed in Plymouth (now Massachusetts). A Wampanoag man named Squanto taught them how to grow food. In 1621 Pilgrims shared their harvest with the Wampanoag at the first thanksgiving.

The 13 English Colonies

By 1733 England had 13 colonies on the coast of North America. Three regions developed different **economies.** Each region used its **natural resources.** The New England Colonies built houses, ships, and barrels from forest wood and fished in their coastal waters. The Middle Colonies made iron tools and grew wheat, selling it to other colonies. The Southern Colonies planted cash crops, such as tobacco and rice, on **plantations.**

Slavery and the Slave Trade

Slavery was a large part of colonial trade. Enslaved Africans were brought to the colonies, sold, and forced to work with no pay. Slave ships followed **triangular trade routes.** By 1760, 40,000 slaves lived in New England and the Middle Colonies, working in homes, inns, and stores. In the South, 250,000 slaves worked on plantations.

The French and Indian War

Conflict over land in the Ohio River Valley led to the **French and Indian War** in 1754. Britain got the land in 1763, after defeating the French and their American Indian allies.

© Scott Foresman Growth of a Nation

Lesson 2: Review

1.  **Summarize** Fill in three details that support the summary below.

By the 1600s, Europeans had established many colonies in North America.

The Dutch founded New Amsterdam in 1624.

2. Identify reasons that European settlers moved to North America.

_____

_____

_____

3. What cash crop was important to Jamestown, and how did it help the colony grow?

_____

_____

_____

4. How was slavery in the New England and Middle Colonies different from slavery in the Southern Colonies?

_____

_____

_____

5. **Critical Thinking:** *Apply Information* Explain how natural resources helped shape the different economies of the New England, Middle, and Southern Colonies.

_____

_____

_____

Lesson 3: Revolution and Constitution

Vocabulary

Stamp Act a law that taxed all printed material in the English colonies

Declaration of Independence a document explaining why the colonists fought for independence from Britain

republic a nation where people elect government representatives

Constitution a written plan for the new American government

checks and balances a system for keeping the balance of power among the three branches of government

Bill of Rights the first ten amendments to the Constitution that state the rights of American citizens

Taxes and Protests

By 1765 all 13 Colonies were self-governed. Since colonists could not vote for representatives in the British government, many believed they should not pay taxes. When Britain passed the **Stamp Act** many colonists protested, "No taxation without representation!" Britain ended the Stamp Act, but still taxed the colonies. Colonists who opposed British rule, called Patriots, united. In 1774 Patriot leaders met at the Continental Congress in Philadelphia and decided to train volunteer armies. Still, most Colonists hoped for a peaceful solution.

Declaring Independence

On April 16, 1775, British soldiers marched to Lexington and Concord to destroy Patriots' weapons. Patriots tried to block them. This fighting began the American Revolution. The Continental Congress formed a Continental Army, led by General George Washington. In June, 1776, a committee started writing the **Declaration of Independence,** explaining the colonies' decision to separate from Britain.

Winning the War

At first, Washington's army lost many battles and faced shortages of soldiers and supplies. In

1777 Americans won the battle of Saratoga, convincing the French to help. Patriot women collected food, raised money, and made clothing for soldiers. There were many heroes. In 1781 the French and the Americans surrounded the British in Yorktown, Virginia and forced them to surrender. The Americans had finally defeated mighty Great Britain.

A New Constitution

American leaders wanted to set up a **republic** and limit the government's power. In 1781 the Continental Congress approved the Articles of Confederation, which set up a weak national government. To create a stronger government, the Congress agreed on a new **Constitution.** It set up three branches of government with a system of **checks and balances** to guard against any one branch becoming too powerful.

The Bill of Rights

Leaders agreed to ten amendments, or additions, called the **Bill of Rights.** These protect freedom of religion, speech, the press, and other rights. The Constitution took effect in 1789. By 1790 all 13 states had approved it.

Lesson 3: Review

1. ⟳ **Summarize** Fill in a sentence that summarizes the details given below.

In 1776 the 13 Colonies declared independence from Great Britain.	In 1781 the United States won the last major battle of the American Revolution.	By 1790 all 13 states approved the United States Constitution.

2. Why did the Stamp Act and other British taxes cause conflict in the 13 Colonies?

_____

_____

_____

3. Name two important decisions made by the Continental Congress in 1775 and 1776.

_____

_____

_____

4. What is one benefit of dividing government into three branches?

_____

_____

_____

5. **Critical Thinking:** *Decision Making* Suppose you were helping to write the Bill of Rights. What are three rights you would want to include?

_____

_____

_____

Lesson 4: A Growing Nation

Vocabulary

Cabinet a group of government leaders who advise the President

political party an organized group of people who share ideas about the role of the government

Industrial Revolution the period of time that introduced making goods by machine, especially in factories

manifest destiny the belief that the United States should expand westward

abolitionist a person who demanded the end of slavery

President Washington

George Washington was elected the first President of the United States in 1789. He divided the Executive Branch into departments. Thomas Jefferson, Secretary of State, handled foreign affairs. Alexander Hamilton managed money matters as the Secretary of the Treasury. These men were part of the President's **Cabinet.** The Cabinet disagreed about the new government. Hamilton believed in a strong government to encourage growth of cities and trade. Jefferson believed in a less powerful government. Each leader organized his own **political party.** After Washington's death in 1799, the capital moved from New York City to a new city named Washington, D.C.

The Louisiana Purchase

Thomas Jefferson became the third President in 1801. In 1803 the U.S. bought the Louisiana Territory from France for $15 million, doubling the size of the country. Jefferson sent Meriwether Lewis and William Clark to explore it. By 1806 they had mapped a vast area, opening the West to new settlers.

The Industrial Revolution

In the 1700s in Britain, people began to make clothing and other goods by machine. Machines made goods faster and more cheaply than by hand. In 1790 Samuel Slater built the first cotton-spinning factory in the United States. New England became the center of the American clothing industry. In 1793 Eli Whitney invented the cotton gin, which could clean 50 times as much cotton as by hand. Several advances in transportation were needed to carry more goods to markets. In 1807 Robert Fulton tested a riverboat powered by a steam engine. In 1830 Peter Cooper built a steam locomotive. By 1840 there were 3,000 miles of railroad. The **Industrial Revolution** changed the way Americans lived and worked.

An Expanding Nation

In the 1820s, American settlers began moving to Texas, which was part of Mexico. Soon the settlers clashed with the Mexican government about how to govern Texas. In 1835 the settlers fought and won independence in the Texas Revolution. Some people wanted to add Texas to the United States, supported by the idea of **manifest destiny.** In the Mexican War, from 1846 to 1848, Mexico gave up most of its northern territory in exchange for $15 million. In 1846 Britain gave The Oregon territory to the United States. The country finally stretched from the Atlantic to the Pacific.

The Abolitionist Movement

As Americans fiercely debated the issue of slavery, **abolitionists** demanded slavery be ended. Many people were inspired by Frederick Douglass, who wrote about his escape from slavery.

Quick Study

Lesson 4: Review

1. **Summarize** Fill in three details that support the summary below.

The federal government moved to Washington, D.C.			

The United States changed in important ways during the first half of the 1800s.

2. What is the President's Cabinet? Describe the role of the Cabinet.

_____

_____

3. What did Lewis and Clark accomplish?

_____

_____

_____

4. How did the Industrial Revolution create the need for better transportation?

_____

_____

_____

5. **Critical Thinking: Compare and Contrast** Describe the different ways the United States gained territory from 1803 to 1848.

_____

_____

_____

Lesson 1: North and South Grow Apart

Vocabulary

sectionalism loyalty to a section or part of the country rather than to the whole country

Two Regions

By the middle 1800s, most Southerners lived and worked on farms and in small towns. There were very few big Southern cities. Most Northerners also lived on farms. However, more and more Northerners were beginning to work in factories and live in large towns and cities. People in the North and South had different economic goals. When Congress passed a tariff law in 1846, Northerners and Southerners had a strong disagreement. The law lowered the tariff, or tax, the United States charged for goods bought from other countries. Northerners did not like this law. Low tariffs meant that people would buy imported goods rather than those made in the North. The Southerners liked this law. They welcomed the lower tariffs. They wanted to buy cheaper goods from other countries, especially Great Britain. These differences caused **sectionalism.** Sectionalism occurs when people are loyal to a section or part of the country rather than to the whole country.

Slavery in the South

The North and South also differed over slavery. Most Northern states did not allow slavery. Northern workers were free. They were paid for their work, though the conditions were often poor and the wages low. Southern states allowed slavery. Slavery was important to the Southern economy. Slave owners made at least twice as much money on goods they sold as it cost them to own slaves. In the South, slaves helped farm cotton, tobacco, and rice on large plantations. About one-third of Southern farmers owned slaves. African Americans suffered from discrimination both in the South and in the North. Even free African Americans did not always have the same voting rights as whites and were not treated as full citizens.

Different Views on Slavery

Abolitionists opposed slavery and believed it should be ended. They believed it was wrong for one human being to own another. Slave owners said that slaves were treated well. They argued that people in Northern factories often worked in poor conditions for little pay. The debate over slavery continued during the middle 1800s.

Lesson 1: Review

1. ⟳ **Main Idea and Details** Complete the graphic organizer to show details supporting the main idea.

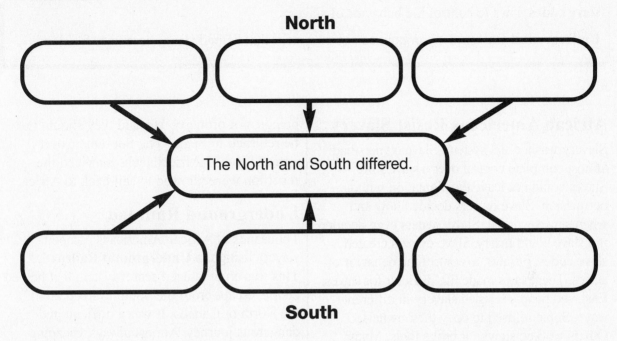

North

The North and South differed.

South

2. Describe how tariffs affected relations between North and South. Use the word **sectionalism** in your answer.

_____

_____

3. In 1860 were more African Americans enslaved or free? How do you know? (Use the chart on page 56 of your textbook.)

_____

_____

4. **Critical Thinking: *Make Inferences*** What conditions existed in the North that might lead to problems at a later date?

_____

_____

5. Describe the main argument of people opposed to slavery.

_____

_____

Lesson 2: Resisting Slavery

Vocabulary

slave codes laws to control the behavior of slaves

Underground Railroad an organized secret system that helped slaves escape to freedom

African Americans Resist Slavery

Slavery was a cruel system. Slave owners had almost complete control over a slave's life. Slaves could not leave the plantation without permission. Slave owners decided how and when slaves worked. Slave owners even decided if a slave could marry. Slave owners created **slave codes,** or laws, to control the behavior of slaves. These laws made life difficult for slaves. Enslaved people resisted slavery in different ways. Some refused to obey their owners. Others worked slowly or broke tools. Many resisted rules that kept them ignorant. Slaves were not allowed to learn to read and write. Some slaves learned in secret. Others risked their lives trying to escape to freedom.

Slave Rebellions

Slave owners tried to keep slaves from meeting so they could not plan rebellions. Still, slave rebellions took place. In August 1831, Nat Turner and his followers killed about 60 whites in Virginia. Soldiers killed more than 100 African Americans before the rebellion ended. Turner was captured and hanged. In 1839 a slave rebellion took place aboard the *Amistad,* a Spanish slave ship. Joseph Cinque led a group of 53 Africans in taking control of the ship. Cinque and his followers tried to return to Africa but were brought instead to the United States. The Africans were taken prisoner. With the help of abolitionists, the Africans fought court battles to gain their freedom. Their case went to the Supreme Court. Former President John Quincy Adams presented the Africans' case. He argued that the Africans were human

beings, not property. He said they should not be returned to Spain. The Supreme Court agreed. The 35 Africans who survived the rebellion were allowed to sail back to Africa.

Underground Railroad

Thousands of African Americans escaped slavery using the **Underground Railroad.** This was an organized secret system that helped people escape from the South to freedom in the North or Canada. It was a difficult and dangerous journey. Almost always, escaping slaves traveled at night. Along the way guides called "conductors" helped them. Slaves hid in houses, barns, and other places called "stations." Harriet Tubman, who had escaped from slavery, was the most famous "conductor." She helped lead more than 300 people to freedom. But not all "conductors" were African Americans. Levi Coffin, a white teacher, and his wife, Catherine, helped more than 2,000 slaves escape.

Free African Americans

By 1860 about 4.5 million African Americans lived in the United States. Most lived in the South and were slaves. Most free African Americans lived in cities. Even though these people were free, many feared losing their freedom. Any white person could accuse an African American of being a slave. African Americans needed a special paper to prove they were free. Without this paper, they could be returned to slavery in the South. Laws and threats made it difficult for free African Americans to find certain jobs. Still, many free blacks found jobs and bought property.

© Scott Foresman Growth of a Nation

Lesson 2: Review

1. 🔄 **Main Idea and Details** Complete the graphic organizer to show the details that support the main idea that enslaved African Americans resisted slavery.

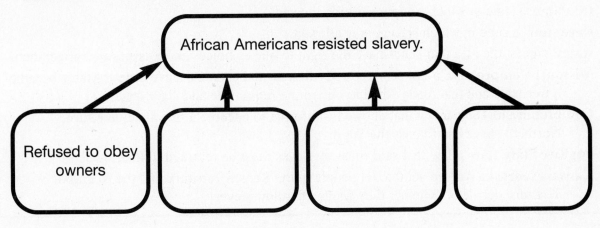

2. What was the purpose of the slave codes?

_____

_____

_____

3. **Critical Thinking:** *Cause and Effect* Why would slave owners want to keep slaves from gathering or meeting one another?

_____

_____

_____

4. Describe how enslaved African Americans escaped to freedom on the Underground Railroad.

_____

_____

_____

5. What challenges were faced by free African Americans in the North and South?

_____

_____

_____

Lesson 3: The Struggle Over Slavery

Vocabulary

free state a state in which slavery was not allowed

slave state a state in which slavery was allowed

states' rights the idea that states have the right to make choices about issues that affect them

Missouri Compromise a law that allowed Missouri to become a slave state if Maine became a free state and that made a line to determine future free and slave states

Compromise of 1850 a law that allowed California to become a free state; in return, Northern states had to pass the Fugitive Slave Law

Fugitive Slave Law a law that said runaway slaves must be returned to their owners

Kansas-Nebraska Act an act that let people in the Kansas Territory and the Nebraska Territory decide on whether they wanted to allow slavery

Missouri Compromise

In 1819 there were 11 **free states** and 11 **slave states.** The people of Missouri asked to become a slave state. Southern states agreed with the people of Missouri. Northern states did not. Some Southern leaders believed in **states' rights** and felt that states should decide whether to allow slavery. The **Missouri Compromise** was a solution. Missouri became a slave state, and Maine became a free state. New states north of a line drawn westward would be free states and those south of it could allow slavery.

The Compromise of 1850

California asked to become a free state in 1849. Then there would be more free states than slave states. **The Compromise of 1850** allowed California to become a free state. In return Northern states had to pass the **Fugitive Slave Law.** The compromise also affected people in the territories won from Mexico. These people could vote on whether they wanted to allow slavery.

"Bleeding Kansas"

In 1854 Nebraska was split into two territories— the Nebraska Territory and the Kansas Territory. Congress passed the **Kansas-Nebraska Act.** The people of Kansas voted for slavery. Many voters

were not from Kansas. Northerners claimed the vote was illegal, and violence broke out.

A Divided Country

Other events caused a deeper split between the North and South. One was the court case of Dred Scott in 1857. Dred Scott was a slave. He claimed he was free. The Supreme Court ruled that he was not free. The court decided that African Americans had no rights. In 1859 an abolitionist named John Brown tried to lead an attack on slave owners in Virginia. He was caught and hanged.

A New Political Party

Ideas about slavery caused the Whig political party to split apart. Members of the Whigs who were against slavery helped form the Republican Party. Abraham Lincoln was a Republican opposed to the spread of slavery. Yet he did not want the country to go to war over slavery.

Lincoln Is Elected President

Abraham Lincoln was elected President in 1860, but he did not get any Southern electoral votes. Southerners were afraid that Lincoln would end slavery. They were also afraid that their opinions would not matter to the new government.

© Scott Foresman Growth of a Nation

Lesson 3: Review

1. ↻ **Main Idea and Details** Complete the graphic organizer with details that support the main idea.

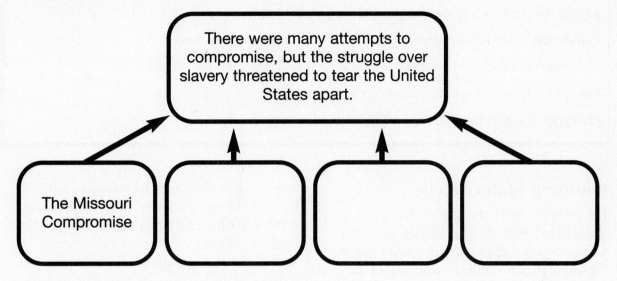

There were many attempts to compromise, but the struggle over slavery threatened to tear the United States apart.

The Missouri Compromise

2. How did the Missouri Compromise keep the balance of free and slave states?

_____

_____

3. How did the Compromise of 1850 affect slavery in California and the territories gained from Mexico?

_____

_____

4. Who were Dred Scott and John Brown? How did their actions affect the split between North and South?

_____

_____

5. **Critical Thinking:** *Make Inferences* What was more important to Abraham Lincoln, abolishing slavery or preserving the nation? Explain.

_____

_____

_____

© Scott Foresman Growth of a Nation

Lesson 4: The First Shots Are Fired

Vocabulary

secede to break away from the government of the rest of the country

Union the states that remained loyal to the United States government

Confederacy the government of the states that seceded from the United States

border state a state located between the Union and Confederate states

civil war a war between people of the same country

Southern States Secede

By February 1861 seven Southern states decided to break away, or **secede,** from the United States. States that remained loyal to the United States government were called the **Union.** South Carolina, Alabama, Florida, Mississippi, Georgia, Louisiana, and Texas seceded. These states formed their own government called the **Confederacy.** The Confederacy created its own constitution. It supported states' rights and slavery. The Confederacy elected Jefferson Davis as its president. Davis was a former United States senator from Mississippi. Davis was concerned that the United States would oppose the Confederacy. When Lincoln became president on March 4, 1861, the Confederacy had taken control of most of the military property in the South. One of the forts still under Union control was Fort Sumter in Charleston, South Carolina.

The War Begins

In April 1861, the Confederates demanded that the Union surrender Fort Sumter. When the fort's commander, Major Robert Anderson, did not immediately surrender, Jefferson Davis ordered Confederate soldiers to attack the fort, starting the Civil War. A **civil war** is a war between people of the same country. Lincoln responded to the attack by sending 75,000 Union soldiers to put down the Confederate rebellion. Lincoln thought it would take about 90 days. Lincoln's call for troops angered people in Virginia, Arkansas, Tennessee, and North Carolina. These four states then joined the Confederacy. There were now 11 states in the Confederacy and 23 in the Union. Four of the Union states—Delaware, Maryland, Missouri, and Kentucky—were slave states. They weren't sure if they wanted to stay in the Union or join the Confederacy. These were called the **border states,** because they were located between the Union and the Confederacy. Lincoln wanted to keep these slave states in the Union, so he said the main reason for fighting the war was to hold the United States together, not to abolish slavery. Still, some Northerners believed that the main purpose of the war was to end slavery. Southerners fought to preserve states' rights and slavery. Some Southerners referred to the conflict as the War for Southern Independence. The war was also called the War Between the States. The Civil War lasted longer and was bloodier than anyone expected.

Lesson 4: Review

1. 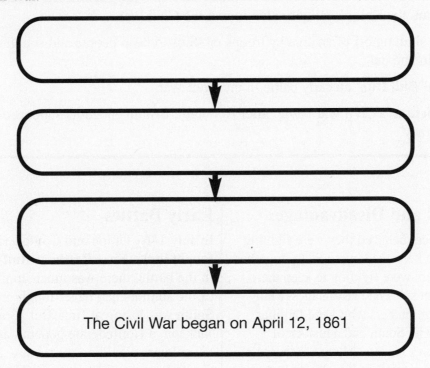 **Sequence** Complete the graphic organizer to show the events that led up to the start of the Civil War.

The Civil War began on April 12, 1861

2. Why did the Southern states secede?

_____

_____

3. **Critical Thinking:** *Draw Conclusions* What might have been Jefferson Davis's reason for attacking Fort Sumter?

_____

_____

4. Describe Abraham Lincoln's main reason for fighting the Civil War.

_____

_____

5. Why at the beginning of the Civil War did Lincoln not say that he was fighting the war to end slavery?

_____

_____

Lesson 1: The Early Stages of the War

Vocabulary

Anaconda Plan the Union's military plan to win the Civil War

blockade the shutting off of an area by troops or ships to keep people and supplies from moving in and out

First Battle of Bull Run an early battle in the Civil War

Battle of Antietam a Civil War battle; after Antietam, Britain ended its support of the Confederacy

Advantages and Disadvantages

Many Northerners believed they were fighting the Civil War to keep the United States together. Most Southerners were fighting to keep their way of life. Both sides had advantages. Many Southerners were hunters who were familiar with weapons. The South had a history of producing military leaders. Many Southerners fought in the Mexican War. The North had more weapons and supplies such as cloth, iron, and wheat. The North also had more ways of moving supplies. It had many more railroads, canals, and roads. The North also raised much more money than the South.

Strategies

General Winfield Scott came up with the **Anaconda Plan** to fight the Confederacy. Just as an anaconda snake squeezes its prey, the Union would squeeze the Confederacy to beat them. First, the Union would set up a **blockade** of the Atlantic and Gulf coasts. The blockade would prevent the Confederacy from selling cotton to Britain to make money for the war. It would also cut off supplies to the South. Second, the Union would gain control over the Mississippi River. This would weaken the South by cutting it in half. Third, the Union would attack the Confederacy from the east and west. The Confederacy thought the Union would get tired and give up. It was also counting on Britain to help fight the Union.

Early Battles

In July 1861 Union and Confederate troops fought in the **First Battle of Bull Run.** Early in the battle, there was much confusion. Most of the soldiers had never fought in a war. The South was losing at first. But "Stonewall" Jackson, a Confederate general, and his soldiers would not turn back. More Confederate soldiers arrived. The Confederacy won, but both sides lost thousands of soldiers. In September 1862 the **Battle of Antietam** was fought. The Union won. After Antietam, Britain decided not to help the Confederacy.

Technology and War

People used new technology during the Civil War. New guns shot farther. Railroads moved troops around more easily. Confederate submarines sailed under Union ship blockades. Soldiers also used early versions of the hand grenade. Both sides used iron-covered ships. The *Virginia* was the Confederacy's iron-covered ship. It battled against the Union's iron-covered ship, the *Monitor*. A huge number of soldiers died because of these new weapons. Medical technology had not advanced far enough to save their lives.

© Scott Foresman Growth of a Nation

Lesson 1: Review

1. 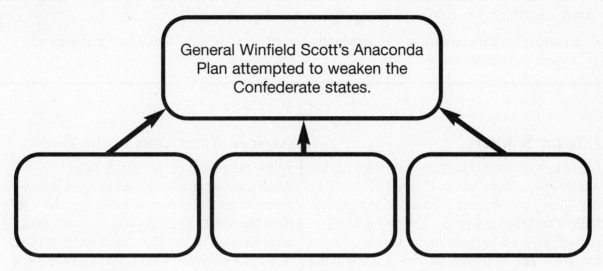 **Main Idea and Details** Complete this chart by filling in the details of the **Anaconda Plan.**

General Winfield Scott's Anaconda Plan attempted to weaken the Confederate states.

2. Compare advantages the Union had at the beginning of the war to those of the Confederacy.

_____

_____

3. How did the strategies of the North and South differ?

_____

_____

4. Summarize the events of the First Battle of Bull Run.

_____

_____

_____

5. **Critical Thinking:** *Analyze Information* What effect did military technology have on Civil War soldiers?

_____

_____

_____

Lesson 2: Life During the War

Vocabulary

draft an order for men of a certain age to serve in the military

Emancipation Proclamation a statement that freed all slaves in Confederate states at war with the Union

Life for Soldiers

Life was hard for soldiers on both sides of the war. Many soldiers marched about 25 miles a day. They carried about 50 pounds of supplies. Many Confederate soldiers did not have enough supplies because of the Union blockade. The **draft** was passed as a law in the North and the South. The draft made men of a certain age serve in the military. Men in the North could pay $300 to get out of the draft. Southern men who owned 20 or more slaves could pay someone to fight in their place. That is why many called the war "a rich man's war and a poor man's fight." Hundreds of thousands of soldiers died on both sides. Most died from disease rather than in battle.

The Emancipation Proclamation

On January 1, 1863, President Lincoln issued the **Emancipation Proclamation.** This statement freed all slaves in Confederate states at war with the Union. Slaves in Confederate states that were already controlled by the Union were not freed. It also did not free slaves in border states. Lincoln believed that he could save the Union by ending slavery. Frederick Douglass was a free African American. He encouraged African Americans to help fight the Confederacy.

African Americans in the War

At the beginning of the war, African Americans were not allowed to fight. Many white Northerners believed that they did not have the ability to fight. African Americans were allowed to join the Union army in 1862. African Americans were not treated the same as white soldiers. They did not get equal pay. In 1863 the African American Massachusetts 54th Regiment led an attack on Fort Wagner in South Carolina. Many soldiers of this regiment died. But they proved to Northerners that they could fight. By June 1864 Congress gave African American and white soldiers equal pay.

Women and the War

Women on both sides helped the war effort. Some women fought or acted as spies. Many women nursed wounded soldiers. Others became teachers, office workers, or ran farms and businesses while their husbands were fighting. Women on both sides lost loved ones in the war. Women in the South also faced shortages of supplies. This made prices in the South rise very high. But both Northern and Southern women made clothing and other supplies that they sent to the armies. They also sent as much food as they could spare.

The War Goes On

By 1863 soldiers on both sides wanted the war to end. They were tired. Their shelter was poor. Many of their friends and family members had died. Many soldiers left the army without permission.

Lesson 2: Review

1. 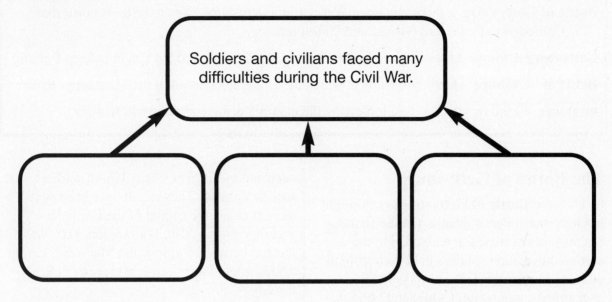 **Main Idea and Details** Complete this chart by filling in the details that support the main idea.

2. Why was the Civil War called a "rich man's war and a poor man's fight"?

    _____

    _____

3. **Critical Thinking:** *Problem Solving* Suppose you had to help President Lincoln decide when to issue the Emancipation Proclamation. How would you solve this problem?

    _____

    _____

4. How did the Massachusetts 54th help change people's minds?

    _____

    _____

5. What role did women play in the Civil War?

    _____

    _____

Lesson 3: How the North Won

Vocabulary

Battle of Gettysburg a three-day Civil War battle; Gettysburg was the farthest north that Confederate forces had pushed into Union territory

Gettysburg Address a speech given by President Lincoln; it inspired the Union to keep fighting

Battle of Vicksburg a Civil War battle in which the Union got control of the Mississippi River

total war a kind of warfare used to destroy the enemy's army and their will to fight

The Battle of Gettysburg

In 1863 the **Battle of Gettysburg** was fought in Gettysburg, Pennsylvania. On the first day, Union soldiers were forced back. On the second day, Union soldiers held their ground on hills. On the third day, both sides exchanged cannon fire. Confederate troops commanded by General George Pickett marched across open ground to attack the well-protected Union troops. The Confederate attack failed. The Southern troops retreated back into Virginia.

The Gettysburg Address

President Lincoln gave a speech called the **Gettysburg Address.** He gave it to honor the soldiers who had died in the war. He wanted to inspire Americans to keep their country together. He said that a united country and an end to slavery were worth fighting for.

The Tide Turns

The Battle of Gettysburg helped turn the tide of the war in favor of the Union. So did other battles. As part of the Anaconda Plan, the Union wanted to gain control of the Mississippi River. They did this at the **Battle of Vicksburg.** In May 1863 the Union blockaded, or closed off, Vicksburg, Mississippi. Confederate soldiers and citizens faced starvation. The Confederacy surrendered Vicksburg on July 4, 1863, one day after the Battle of Gettysburg ended. The largest number of Civil War battles occurred in Virginia. Many Union soldiers were sent to Virginia. They might have been sent there because the capital of the Confederacy was in Virginia. Also, Washington, D.C. was located between Virginia and Maryland. Union troops might have been sent there to defend the city.

The War Ends

Union General William Tecumseh Sherman helped wear down the Confederate army. He used **total war** to destroy the Confederate soldiers' will to fight. First, Sherman and his troops took Atlanta, Georgia, an important industrial and railway center. Sherman's army marched to take over Savannah, Georgia. They destroyed everything in their path that the South could use to keep fighting. This is called Sherman's "March to the Sea." The Confederacy surrendered in Virginia on April 9, 1865. General Lee and General Grant met in a farmhouse in Appomattox Court House, Virginia, to discuss the terms of surrender. The Civil War was the most destructive war in American history. President Lincoln wanted the country to join together and rebuild itself.

© Scott Foresman Growth of a Nation

Lesson 3: Review

1. 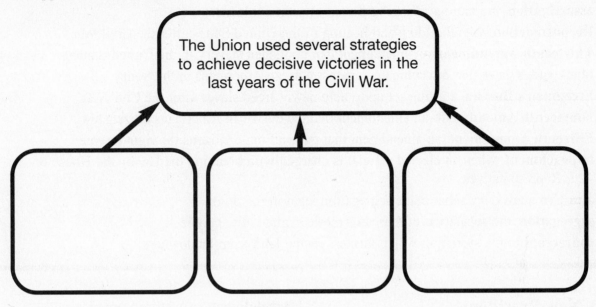 **Main Idea and Details** Complete this chart by filling in the missing details that support the main idea.

The Union used several strategies to achieve decisive victories in the last years of the Civil War.

2. What circumstances led the Union to victory on the third day in the Battle of Gettysburg?

_____

_____

3. What were Lincoln's goals as expressed in the Gettysburg Address?

_____

_____

4. **Critical Thinking:** *Interpret Maps* Look at the map on page 99 of your textbook. In what state did most of the major battles occur in the Civil War? Give a reason you think this would be so.

_____

_____

_____

5. What was the purpose of total war and Sherman's "March to the Sea"?

_____

_____

_____

Lesson 4: The End of Slavery

Vocabulary

assassination the murder of a government or political leader

Reconstruction the rebuilding and healing of the United States after the Civil War

Thirteenth Amendment an amendment that abolished slavery in the United States

black codes laws that discriminated against African Americans in the South

Freedmen's Bureau a group set up to help newly freed slaves after the Civil War

Fourteenth Amendment an amendment that gave African Americans citizenship

Fifteenth Amendment an amendment that gave all male citizens the right to vote

impeachment when an elected official is charged with breaking the law by the House of Representatives

Jim Crow laws laws that made segregation legal in the South

segregation the separation of African American and white people

sharecropping a system in which farmers rented land from landowners

A New President

On April 15, 1865, President Lincoln was **assassinated.** Vice-President Andrew Johnson became President. He wanted to carry out Lincoln's plan for **Reconstruction.** The **Thirteenth Amendment** abolished slavery across the nation on December 18, 1865. Confederate states were to become part of the Union again. Under Johnson's Reconstruction plan, Southern states could pass **black codes.** Black codes took away many rights from African American men. Republican members of Congress did not trust Johnson's Reconstruction plan. They thought it was too easy on the South.

Reconstruction Under Congress

In 1867 Congress passed the first of several Reconstruction Acts. These laws made Southern states give African American men the right to vote. People who were Confederate officers or leaders could not vote or hold office. Congress also set up the **Freedmen's Bureau.** Many white Southerners were angry about the laws.

New Amendments

To be readmitted to the Union, Southern states had to accept two amendments. The **Fourteenth** **Amendment** gave African Americans citizenship. It also said that laws must protect all citizens equally. The **Fifteenth Amendment** gave all male citizens, including African American males, the right to vote. President Johnson fought the Fourteenth Amendment and Reconstruction laws. Congress wanted to remove him from office by **impeachment.**

Reconstruction Ends

By 1870 all former Confederate states were readmitted to the Union. New state laws were passed that took away the rights of African Americans. Some states required African Americans to pay a poll tax in order to vote. Some places made African Americans pass a reading test before they could vote. **Jim Crow laws** also **segregated,** or separated, African Americans and whites in public places. Many farmers started **sharecropping.** Many people fell into debt under this system. The end of Reconstruction opened a new phase in American history. The era of slavery was over. The federal government had established power over individual states. The new amendments provided a basis for equal rights, but it would be a long time before they were fully recognized.

Lesson 4: Review

1. 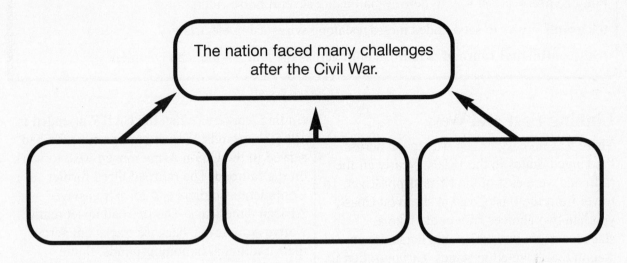 **Main Idea and Details** Complete this chart by filling in the details that support the main idea.

The nation faced many challenges after the Civil War.

2. Why did Republicans in Congress dislike Johnson's Reconstruction plan?

_____

_____

_____

3. **Critical Thinking:** *Cause and Effect* How did the Reconstruction Acts affect the South?

_____

_____

4. Why were three amendments added to the Constitution during Reconstruction?

_____

_____

5. How were the lives of African Americans made more difficult after the end of Reconstruction? Use the word segregation in your answer.

_____

_____

© Scott Foresman Growth of a Nation

Lesson 1: Rails Across the Nation

Vocabulary

Pony Express a fast way to deliver mail using several horse riders

telegraph a way to send coded messages along wires using electricity

transcontinental railroad a railroad built across the North American continent

Linking East and West

There was no easy or fast way to get across the United States in the 1850s. Nearly all the railroads were east of the Mississippi River. To travel from the East Coast to the West Coast, you had two choices. You could take a stagecoach, an uncomfortable horse-drawn wagon that traveled in stages. Or you sailed to Panama in Central America, crossed Panama by train, then sailed north to California. In 1860 the **Pony Express** began delivering mail from Missouri to California. The Pony Express was like a 2,000-mile relay race. Each rider rode about 75 miles, then handed his mail bags to the next rider. Riders changed horses every 10 or 15 miles. In 1861 the first telegraph line across the country was completed. The **telegraph,** developed by Samuel Morse, put the Pony Express out of business. Using Morse Code, messages could be sent coast to coast in a few minutes.

The Transcontinental Railroad

Many people believed the best way to link the East and West would be to build a **transcontinental railroad.** In 1862 the United States government hired two companies to build it. The Union Pacific began building track west from Omaha, Nebraska. The Central Pacific began building track east from Sacramento, California.

Across the Plains

The government paid the two companies in land and money for every mile of track completed. At first, the Union Pacific, far from big towns and cities, had a hard time finding workers. When the Civil War ended in 1865, thousands of Irish immigrants who had served in the Union Army moved west to work on the railroad. The railroad hired former Confederate soldiers and former enslaved African Americans. The railroad upset many Native Americans, because tracks cut across their traditional hunting grounds. Some groups, like the Lakota and Cheyenne, complained that the railroad scared away the buffalo. The Union Pacific was determined to continue, supported by the United States government.

Over the Mountains

Young Chinese immigrants who came to California to search for gold were often treated unfairly at the gold mining camps. Many joined the Central Pacific workforce. They did the dangerous work of blasting though the mountains. Many were killed, but work never stopped. The work went more quickly once the tracks were completed through the mountains in 1867. The transcontinental railroad was a source of great national excitement and pride.

The Golden Spike

The railroad was completed on May 19, 1869. The tracks of the Union Pacific and Central Pacific met at Promontory Point, Utah. To celebrate, a golden spike was driven into them. Now a transcontinental trip could be made in a week for less than $100.

© Scott Foresman Growth of a Nation

Lesson 1: Review

1. ↻ **Sequence** Complete the chart by filling in key events from this lesson in the order they happened.

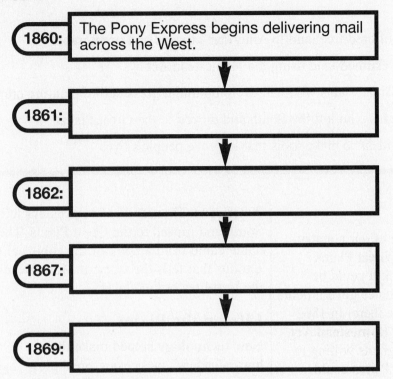

1860: The Pony Express begins delivering mail across the West.

↓

1861:

↓

1862:

↓

1867:

↓

1869:

2. Why did new telegraph lines put the Pony Express out of business?

_____

_____

3. Describe two problems faced by the Union Pacific railroad.

_____

_____

4. What role did Chinese workers play in building the Central Pacific railroad?

_____

_____

5. **Critical Thinking:** *Predict* Suppose you lived in the United States in 1869. What kinds of changes would you expect the new transcontinental railroad to bring?

_____

_____

Lesson 2: Pioneers on the Plains

Vocabulary

pioneer a new settler

Homestead Act a law that offered free land to American citizens and immigrants

homesteader a settler who claimed land using the Homestead Act

sodbuster a farmer in the Great Plains who had to rip up tough grass before planting crops

exodusters African Americans who left the South and moved to the Great Plains

technology the use of new ideas to make tools that improve people's lives

The Great Plains

In the mid-1800s, the middle of our country was dry grassland called the Great Plains. Many Americans did not think it could be good farmland. The United States government encouraged **pioneers** to move there. In 1862 President Lincoln signed the **Homestead Act.** American citizens and immigrants willing to start new farms on the Great Plains could claim 160 acres of land for about $10. If they farmed the land and lived on it for five years, they owned the land. These settlers were called **homesteaders.**

Settling on the Plains

Great Plains farmers were called **sodbusters** as they had to "bust" through the "sod" and rip up the grass. Sod was useful for building houses, because the region had few trees. These houses stayed cool in the summer and warm in the winter, and were fireproof. The soil of the Great Plains was actually very good for planting.

America Fever

News of the fertile soil spread across Europe. Thousands of families came from Germany, Sweden, Norway, Russia, and other countries, bringing their own farming skills. Farmers from Russia brought seeds for a strong wheat. The Homestead Act also helped African Americans. Thousands of **exodusters** left the South and moved to the Great Plains. The name came from a book of the Bible called Exodus that tells the story of Moses leading the Israelites out of slavery.

Life on the Plains

New **technology** helped make the homesteaders' lives easier. Steel plows helped settlers plow the thick soil. Windmills pumped underground water to the surface and created power. Barbed wire was an easy and cheap material for building fences. But harsh weather and natural disasters often struck the Great Plains. Blizzards, tornadoes, hailstorms, flooding, and fires came with the changing seasons. Farmers also faced the dreaded grasshopper who could destroy everything from crops to fences.

Growth in the West

Many people moved even farther west. New railroad lines brought thousands of people to Washington, Oregon, and California. Towns such as Seattle and Los Angeles quickly grew into important cities. The West also attracted farmers from other countries. In the late 1800s, thousands of Japanese immigrants arrived in California. Many built successful farms in the West.

© Scott Foresman Growth of a Nation

Lesson 2: Review

1. 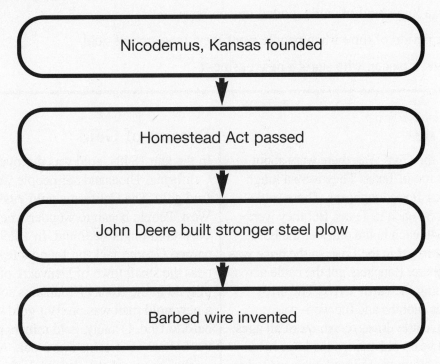**Sequence** Redraw this diagram by putting the events in their correct order. Include the year of each event.

Nicodemus, Kansas founded

↓

Homestead Act passed

↓

John Deere built stronger steel plow

↓

Barbed wire invented

2. What did the government hope the Homestead Act would accomplish?

_____

_____

3. Who were the exodusters? What caused them to move to the Great Plains?

_____

_____

4. Describe two inventions that helped pioneers on the Great Plains.

_____

_____

5. **Critical Thinking:** *Decision Making* You know about the difficulties of living and farming on the Great Plains. Would you have wanted to be a homesteader? Use the Decision Making steps on page H3 of your textbook.

_____

_____

© Scott Foresman Growth of a Nation

Lesson 3: Cowboys and Miners

Vocabulary

cattle drive a huge herd of cattle guided by cowboys

gold rush a period of time when people went West in search of gold

entrepreneur a person who starts a new business

Cowboy Life

By the end of the Civil War, there were about five million cattle in Texas. They were a tough breed known as Texas longhorns. These cattle sold for about $4 each in Texas. But they were worth about $40 each in the cities of the East. Beef was hard to get in the East, so the price was much higher there. Ranchers got the cattle across the country using the **cattle drive.** The drive could last three months and the work was dangerous. On cattle drives, cowboys of all ages, from 15 to 69 years old, guided the huge herds north to towns along the railroad, such as Dodge City, Kansas. From these towns, cattle were taken by train to eastern cities. About a third of all cowboys were Mexican American or African American.

The End of the Drives

Cattle drives came to an end in the late 1800s. One cause was the conflict between cattle ranchers and farmers on the Great Plains. Farmers didn't want cattle crossing their farmlands, so they fenced in their lands with barbed wire. As new railroad lines reached into Texas, it was no longer necessary to drive cattle north. Still, people all over the country wanted fresh meat at good prices. Ranchers raised millions of cows, hogs, and sheep to meet the demand. As railroad lines expanded, it became easier and cheaper to transport the animals. Chicago, Illinois, a major railroad center near the middle of the country, became the nation's leading supplier of meat.

Dreams of Gold

In the late 1840s, gold was discovered in California. Thousands of people went there to find gold. The California **gold rush** changed the West. People began to wonder where else in the West gold might be found. In 1859 a miner named George Jackson found a few gold flakes near the small town of Denver, Colorado. News of gold in the Rocky Mountains soon spread and a new gold rush was on. But gold was rare and hard to find. Usually, gold miners put sand from the bottom of streams into a pan. As they washed the sand out, they looked carefully for pieces of gold called "gold dust." Gold dust was taken to the nearest town to be traded for supplies or deposited in a bank.

Boom Towns and Blue Jeans

Miners rushed to any place where gold was found. Mining camps grew into booming towns. These "boom towns" offered opportunities to **entrepreneurs.** Some entrepreneurs in mining towns opened restaurants. Levi Strauss, an entrepreneur from Germany, saw that miners needed sturdy pants. He began making pants out of blue denim, held together with rivets, or metal pins. These were the world's first blue jeans. After gold and silver were discovered in Virginia City, Nevada, the small mining camp became one of the West's biggest boom towns. But when there was no more gold and silver left to mine, people left. Even Virginia City became a "ghost town." Still, the mining boom had a lasting effect. Thousands of settlers stayed, and important cities grew up.

© Scott Foresman Growth of a Nation

Lesson 3: Review

1. ↻ **Sequence** Complete the chart by filling in the missing dates in this time line.

Date   **Event**

: Gold is found in the Rocky Mountains.

: Mark Twain moves to Virginia City.

: The Goodnight-Loving trail is established.

: Nat Love becomes a cowboy.

2. Why did ranchers decide to drive their cattle from Texas to towns along the railroad?

_____

_____

3. What changes brought cattle drives to an end?

_____

_____

4. Summarize the lasting effect of the search for gold in the West.

_____

_____

5. **Critical Thinking:** *Analyze Primary Sources* Read Mark Twain's description of life in Virginia City (page 152 of your textbook). List three details that Twain uses to give the reader an idea of what life was like in Virginia City.

_____

_____

Lesson 4: War in the West

Vocabulary

reservation an area of land set aside for Native Americans

Battle of Little Bighorn the battle in which General Custer was defeated by the Lakota and Cheyenne

Conflict on the Plains

Thousands of settlers moved into the Great Plains in the 1860s. This led to conflicts between settlers and Native American groups, such as the Lakota, Cheyenne, and Crow. The Native Americans saw that their traditional way of life was threatened. The U.S. government wanted more railroads, farms, and ranches in the region. Government leaders decided to move Native Americans onto **reservations.** Realizing they could not defeat the U. S. Army, many Native Americans agreed to move. In 1868 the United States signed a treaty with the Lakota, giving them a large reservation in what is now South Dakota and Wyoming. Then in 1874, gold was found in the Black Hills on the Great Lakota Reservation. Thousands of miners illegally rushed onto Lakota land. The United States wanted to buy the Black Hills from the Lakota and even threatened the Lakota. But the Lakota refused to sell.

The Battle of Little Bighorn

Colonel George Custer and the Seventh Cavalry were sent to force the Lakota onto a new reservation. On June 25, 1876, Custer found Chief Sitting Bull and the Lakota camped on the banks of the Little Bighorn River in Montana. Crazy Horse, one of the Lakota's best warriors, was there too, along with Cheyenne fighters. Though American soldiers were badly outnumbered, Custer attacked anyway. The **Battle of Little Bighorn** is also known as "Custer's Last Stand." Custer and his entire force of more than 200 soldiers were killed. The U.S. government sent more soldiers to the

Great Plains. By 1877, Crazy Horse and most of the Lakota had been forced onto reservations. Sitting Bull escaped to Canada. The Black Hills were opened to miners and settlers.

Chief Joseph

Chief Joseph was the leader of the Nez Percé, in Oregon. The United States government wanted them to move to a reservation in Idaho Territory. Many Nez Percé did not want to leave their traditional land. After many battles, they tried to escape to Canada, to Sitting Bull's camp. But 40 miles from Canada, they were surrounded by American soldiers. Although the government promised Chief Joseph that if he surrendered, the Nez Percé would be allowed to return to Oregon, the promise was not kept. The Nez Percé were taken to a reservation in Oklahoma.

After the Wars

The Apache continued fighting into the 1880s. Their leader was Geronimo, who was finally forced to surrender in 1886. The last major conflict between United States soldiers and Native Americans took place in 1890. At Wounded Knee, South Dakota, a group of Lakota families who had decided to leave their reservation were surrounded by soldiers who killed about 300 Lakota. Native Americans had to adjust to life on reservations. Today about half of the 2.5 million Native Americans live on or near reservations. Native Americans are educating young people, writing stories, and creating films to keep their history alive.

© Scott Foresman Growth of a Nation

Lesson 4: Review

1. 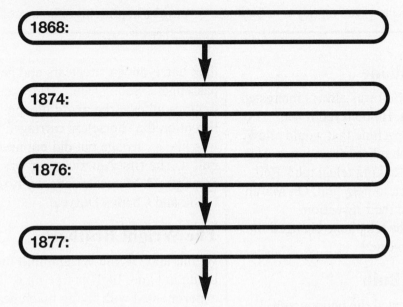 **Sequence** Create a time line of the struggle of the Native Americans for their land. Fill in one key event for each year shown.

1868:

1874:

1876:

1877:

2. What changes threatened the way of life for Native Americans of the Great Plains in the 1860s?

_____

_____

3. Why was the Battle of Little Bighorn important?

_____

_____

4. What are some ways in which Native Americans are keeping their traditions alive today?

_____

_____

5. **Critical Thinking:** *Summarize* Summarize the outcome of the wars between United States forces and Native Americans.

_____

_____

Lesson 1: Inventors Change the World

Vocabulary

investor a person who gives money to a business or project hoping to make a profit

The First Telephone

Alexander Graham Bell was always interested in sound and speech. He believed it was possible to make a machine that would allow people to talk to each other across wires. He called this idea the "talking telegraph." Bell hired Thomas Watson to help him. On March 10, 1876, they tested their invention successfully. Soon the telephone changed the way people communicated.

Edison's Light Bulb

Thomas Edison invented the phonograph. He also wanted to build an electric light bulb, so he raised money to pay for his experiments from **investors.** Edison did many experiments with filaments. In 1879 Edison and his team built a bulb with a carbon filament that glowed for two days. An African American inventor, Lewis Latimer, invented a way to make carbon filaments last longer. This invention helped make electric light practical for everyday use.

Electricity Brings Change

Thomas Edison knew that electric light could change life in the United States. He decided to build a power station in New York City. He began testing the power station in the summer of 1882. When he turned the power station on, lights in 40 different buildings began glowing. Soon other cities built power stations of their own. The number of homes with electricity began rising quickly in the 1900s.

Streetcars and Horseless Carriages

Richmond, Virginia, had the first system of electric streetcars to replace the old horse-drawn streetcars. They traveled more quickly than horse-drawn streetcars and held more passengers. Soon electric streetcars were built in cities all over the world. People called the invention the "horseless carriage," because it was like a carriage but did not need a horse to pull it. The first American car was built in Springfield, Massachusetts, by two brothers, Frank and Charles Duryea.

The Wright Brothers

Wilbur and Orville Wright built bicycles for a living in Ohio. In their free time, the brothers experimented with flying machines. They practiced with gliders at a beach in Kitty Hawk, North Carolina. They had many failures, but kept trying. They built a plane called *Flyer* and designed a light-weight motor and propeller. *Flyer* actually flew about 120 feet on December 17, 1903. The flight lasted only 12 seconds, but it was the first time that a machine carrying a person raised itself by its own power and flew.

Inventions and Industry

The inventions you have read about all led to new industries. People started businesses to offer telephone service and electrical service. They created companies to make streetcars, automobiles, and airplanes. In 1910 a woman named Blanche Stuart Scott drove a car across the country to advertise a car company. The trip made her famous. She was hired to fly airplanes at fairs for the Curtiss Airplane and Motor Company. Scott was the first American woman to fly an airplane.

Lesson 1: Review

1. **Sequence** Redraw this chart by putting the events in their correct order. Include the year of each event.

```
┌──────────────────────────────────┐
│   The Wright Brothers make the    │
│    world's first airplane flight. │
└──────────────────────────────────┘
                 ↓
┌──────────────────────────────────┐
│  The first electric streetcar system │
│    opens in Richmond, Virginia.   │
└──────────────────────────────────┘
                 ↓
┌──────────────────────────────────┐
│      Thomas Edison opens a        │
│    power plant in New York City.  │
└──────────────────────────────────┘
                 ↓
┌──────────────────────────────────┐
│     The Duryea Brothers build the │
│    first car in the United States.│
└──────────────────────────────────┘
```

2. How did Alexander Graham Bell's invention affect communication in the United States?

_____

_____

3. What are two important inventions for which Thomas Edison is remembered?

_____

_____

4. Describe three inventions that changed the way people traveled.

_____

_____

5. **Critical Thinking: *Cause and Effect*** How did inventions such as the telephone, electric light, and car lead to the rise of new industries?

_____

_____

Lesson 2: The Rise of Big Business

Vocabulary

corporation a business owned by investors

stock a share or shares in a company sold to investors

monopoly a company that has control of an entire industry

free enterprise a system in which people are free to start their own businesses and own
property

consumer a person who buys or uses goods and services

human resource a person with knowledge or skill

capital resource the tools and machines that companies use to produce goods and services;
money used to buy equipment

Building with Steel

Steel is made by heating iron until it melts and then adding carbon. Steel is much stronger than iron. An entrepreneur named Andrew Carnegie bought iron and coal mines to develop steel mills. He bought ships and railroads to move his steel and supplies. Carnegie helped steel become a major industry in the early 1900s.

Railroads Link Markets

By 1893, the United States had 160,000 miles of railroad track. Railroad companies became the nation's first large corporations. A **corporation** is a business owned by investors. A corporation sells shares of the company, called **stocks,** to investors. The corporation can then use the money to do things such as buying equipment. Railroads linked cities, farms, factories, and mines all over the United States and helped the economy grow.

The Oil Industry

Because of its value, oil was sometimes called "black gold." John D. Rockefeller was an entrepreneur who built his first oil refinery in Cleveland, Ohio, in 1863. He used the profits to buy other refineries. His company, Standard Oil

Company, became larger and larger, slowly gaining control of the nation's oil industry. By the 1880s, Standard Oil was a monopoly. A **monopoly** has control of an entire industry and can charge any price it wants for its products.

Free Enterprise

The United States economy is based on **free enterprise.** People are free to start their own businesses, own property, and decide what to produce and how much to charge. **Consumers** are free to buy what they want. Companies compete for their business. Westinghouse Electric Company competed with Thomas Edison's electric company. People thought Westinghouse had the better product and that company grew into a large corporation.

Resources and Big Business

The United States is rich in natural resources important to industry. **Human resources** increased, and bankers like J.P. Morgan supplied money, a kind of **capital resource.**

Help Wanted

By 1900, more Americans worked in industries than on farms. Many people from rural areas and other countries moved to cities for jobs.

© Scott Foresman Growth of a Nation

Lesson 2: Review

1. ⟳ **Main Idea and Details** Complete the chart below by filling in three details about the rise of big business in the United States.

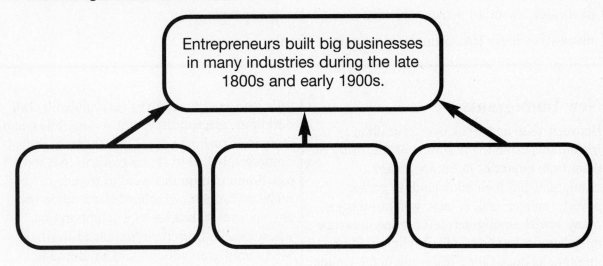

Entrepreneurs built big businesses in many industries during the late 1800s and early 1900s.

2. How was Andrew Carnegie able to produce huge amounts of steel at low prices?

_____

_____

3. How did railroads help the United States economy grow?

_____

_____

4. What freedoms do business owners and consumers have in a free enterprise system?

_____

_____

5. **Critical Thinking:** *Cause and Effect* What are some ways that the rise of big business changed the United States?

_____

_____

Lesson 3: New Americans

Vocabulary

prejudice an unfair negative opinion about a group of people

diversity variety (for example, in a group of people)

New Immigrants

Between 1880 and 1920, over 23 million immigrants came to the United States, many of them from countries in Europe. Many immigrants left their homelands to escape poverty, hunger, lack of jobs, war, or injustice. Many Jewish immigrants left Europe to escape mistreatment because of their religion. Most immigrants hoped for a better life in the United States for themselves and their families.

Ellis Island

Most ships carrying immigrants from Europe landed in New York and were taken by ferry boat to Ellis Island. Immigrants had to go there to get permission to enter the country. At Ellis Island, doctors checked immigrants for dangerous diseases. Government workers asked immigrants questions about where the immigrants were from, what kind of work they did, and where they planned to live.

Angel Island

In the early 1900s, many immigrants came to the United States from China. They were held at Angel Island in San Francisco Bay because a law limited the number of Chinese immigrants. To get permission, most Chinese immigrants had to prove they had family members already living in the United States. Until then, they had to stay on Angel Island for weeks or even months.

A New World

For many immigrants, arriving in a big American city in the late 1800s and early 1900s was like stepping into a different world. Immigrants who came from small farming villages found themselves surrounded by tall buildings, electric streetcars, automobiles, and crowds of rushing people. Most recent arrivals immediately had to find a place to live and a job. Some immigrants went to friends or relatives for help. People who did not know anyone usually headed to a neighborhood where people from their homeland lived. Many immigrants found jobs in railroads, factories, and mines. Others started their own businesses. If people did not have enough money to open a store, they could sell goods from a pushcart on the streets. Many immigrants faced prejudice. **Prejudice** is an unfair negative opinion about a group of people. Most immigrants had to work long hours to make a living. Many of them went to school at night, because they realized that education was one of the keys to a better life.

Immigration and Diversity

By the early 1900s, more than half the people living in most big American cities were immigrants or the children of immigrants. More people of Irish background lived in New York City than in Dublin, Ireland's largest city. Los Angeles, California, had the world's second largest Mexican population. Only Mexico City, Mexico, had a larger one. Immigrants contributed to the **diversity,** or variety, of the American population. In 1924 the United States government passed laws that limited the number of immigrants who could enter the country each year.

© Scott Foresman Growth of a Nation

Lesson 3: Review

1. ⏱ **Summarize** Complete the chart below by filling in reasons that immigrants came to the United States.

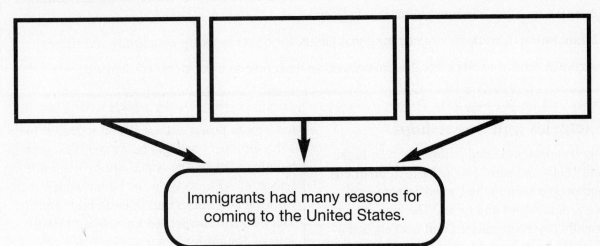

Immigrants had many reasons for coming to the United States.

2. How were Ellis Island and Angel Island similar? How were they different?

_____

_____

3. How did prejudice create problems for some immigrants in the late 1800s and early 1900s?

_____

_____

4. Why did the period of largely unregulated immigration come to an end in the 1920s?

_____

_____

5. **Critical Thinking:** *Express Ideas* Why do you think so many people were willing to face the challenge of starting new lives in the United States?

_____

_____

Lesson 4: The Labor Movement

Vocabulary

sweatshop a hot, cramped room in a factory

labor union a workers' organization that fights for better working conditions and wages

strike a refusal to work because business owners refuse to meet workers' demands

Factories and Sweatshops

Big businesses created millions of jobs in the late 1800s and early 1900s. Many immigrants and people born in the United States found work in factories and mines. The jobs did not usually pay good salaries, and workers had to work 12-hour days. Many women worked in clothing factories in cramped rooms known as **sweatshops,** where they earned even less money. Sweatshops could also be dangerous places to work. Workers at the Triangle Shirtwaist Company were worried about their safety, because the building had no fire escapes, and the doors were usually locked. The owners did not improve conditions, and in March 1911, a fire killed 146 people at the Triangle factory.

Children at Work

In 1900 about 2 million children under age 16 had to work to help support their families. Many worked in textile mills, where the conditions were often dangerous and unhealthy. In coal mining towns, young children often worked as "breaker boys," sitting on benches and sorting through coal to get rid of rocks, breathing in coal dust all day. Children usually worked 12 or more hours a day for just 10 to 20 cents. There was no time for school.

Labor Unions

Many workers joined **labor unions** to fight for better working conditions and wages. Samuel Gompers was an early union leader who led union workers to **strike,** or refuse to work, if business owners refused to meet their demands. Gompers realized that unions would

have more power if they joined together. In 1886 Gompers brought many workers' unions together to form the American Federation of Labor, or AFL, to fight for better wages and working conditions and to end child labor. Mary Harris Jones, also known as "Mother Jones," fought for better working conditions for coal miners until she was in her 90s.

Going on Strike

There were tensions between striking workers and business owners. Sometimes the tensions led to violence. This happened at the Homestead Steel Works in 1892. With the price of steel falling, the company owners decided to lower wages. The workers did not think this was fair, and they went on strike. People on both sides were killed. However, most strikes were settled peacefully. The strike in 1899 by "newsies," or children who sold newspapers, was ended when the newsies reached a fair agreement with the newspaper owners.

Improving Conditions

Labor unions, religious organizations, political leaders, and even business owners improved life for workers. New laws shortened working hours and improved workplace conditions. Unions also succeeded in creating a new holiday—Labor Day. The first Labor Day celebration was held in September 1882. In 1894 Congress declared Labor Day to be an official national holiday, which we now celebrate on the first Monday in September.

© Scott Foresman Growth of a Nation

Lesson 4: Review

1. ⊚ **Draw Conclusions** Complete the chart by filling in a conclusion that could be drawn from the information given.

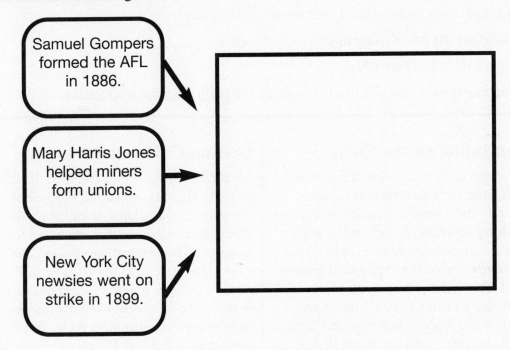

Samuel Gompers formed the AFL in 1886.

Mary Harris Jones helped miners form unions.

New York City newsies went on strike in 1899.

2. What conditions led to the rise of labor unions?

_____

_____

3. What were the main goals of labor unions such as the AFL?

_____

_____

4. In what ways did conditions begin to improve for workers in the early 1900s?

_____

_____

5. **Critical Thinking:** *Evaluate* Why do you think a disaster like the Triangle Shirtwaist Factory fire might have encouraged people to join unions?

_____

_____

Lesson 1: Rural Life Changes

Vocabulary

manual labor work done by hand, without the help of machines

mechanization the act of using machines to do work

reaper a machine that cuts wheat

threshing machine a machine used to separate the grain from the plant stalks

Mechanization on the Farm

Farming in the early 1800s was difficult and tiring and done with **manual labor.** Then farmers and others invented machines, such as the **threshing machine,** to help make work easier, called **mechanization.** In 1834 Cyrus McCormick perfected the mechanical **reaper** which did the work of 16 workers. Machines also made dairy farming easier and helped farmers do more work in less time and farm more of their land. Farms increased in size, and farmers could grow "cash crops," for profit instead of just to feed their families. With the money they made, farmers could buy even more land.

Industry's Impact

Industry was growing in cities like New York and Chicago. Factories made buckets, birdcages, clothing, and even tractors and washing machines. Stores sold things to people in cities. But not everyone lived near cities. In the 1800s, many Americans lived on farms and ranches, where they made their own clothes, soap, and furniture. In 1872 Aaron Montgomery Ward established the first mail-order business in Chicago, helping farmers to buy factory-made items that were shipped across the country by train. In 1893 Richard Sears and Alvah C. Roebuck formed another mail-order company that grew to be even larger than Montgomery Ward's.

Getting Connected

Alexander Graham Bell invented the telephone in 1876. He also owned the first telephone company. Soon, telephone poles and lines spread across the country. Phones were installed in homes and businesses. But it cost a lot to install a large phone system. Phone rates were high. It was very expensive to install a phone system in rural areas as there weren't enough customers there. In 1893 Bell's patent expired. Other companies could now build and install phone systems. Small companies began to form in rural areas. Farmers also banded together to put up their own phone lines, ordering building materials and telephones by mail-order.

Electrifying the Countryside

The first hydroelectric plant, or factory, was opened in 1882. Hydroelectric power plants use running water to make electricity. Power stations brought electricity to homes and factories. But people who lived far from power plants had to wait to get electricity, sometimes for years. Many farmers had to rely on wind power, water power, machine power, and their own power to get work done. In 1936 the Rural Electrification Act was passed, and the government loaned money to states to create and improve electrical service in rural areas. Electricity improved life in rural areas, from electric water pumps, to electric lights, to electric appliances such as vacuums and washing machines.

© Scott Foresman Growth of a Nation

Name _____ Date _____

Lesson 1: Review

1. 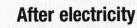 **Compare and Contrast** Complete the chart by filling in the boxes to contrast rural people's lives before and after the arrival of electricity.

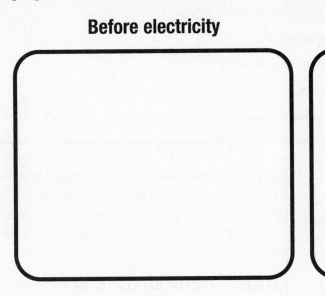

Before electricity   **After electricity**

2. How did advances in mechanization affect farm life in the late 1800s? Use the highlighted word in your answer.

_____

_____

3. How did the growth of industry make it easier for farmers to get goods?

_____

_____

4. Why did big cities have new services such as telephone systems and electricity before rural areas did?

_____

_____

5. **Critical Thinking:** *Draw Conclusions* Why do you think people in the 1880s were so eager to have telephones?

_____

_____

Lesson 2: Life in the Growing Cities

Vocabulary

urbanization the movement of people from rural areas to cities

tenement a building divided into small apartments

settlement house a center that provides help for the poor

political machine an organization that controls votes to gain political power

suspension bridge a bridge that is suspended, or hung, from steel cables

Growing Cities

In the late 1800s and early 1900s, the United States became a nation of city dwellers. Cities such as New York, Chicago, and Philadelphia grew rapidly.

Immigration and Urbanization

Most immigrants who came to the United States between 1890 and 1910 moved to cities. This was also a time of rapid **urbanization.** Some people lived in **tenements** and cities became ugly and crowded. In the 1890s, a "city beautiful movement" began. Parks and playgrounds were built but not fast enough. Transportation both solved and created problems. Streetcars, subways, and automobiles meant workers could live farther from their jobs, but traffic problems grew.

Urban Woes

Uncontrolled growth in cities created many problems. Tenements were unsafe and uncomfortable. Diseases spread, causing concern about public health. In 1918 a huge outbreak of influenza killed more than 500,000 Americans. Immigrants seen as "different," faced prejudice when looking for work.

Seeking Solutions

Many organizations tried to solve the cities' problems, including the YMCA, YMHA, and the Salvation Army, all of which still exist

today. In 1889 Jane Addams founded Hull House, a **settlement house,** in Chicago. Immigrants took English classes there and children received day care. Settlement houses opened in other cities.

Rise of Political Machines

City governments had trouble handling urban problems and many people were unhappy. **Political machines** formed to take advantage of this unhappiness. They wanted to get their candidates elected. They promised immigrants homes and jobs in exchange for votes. But the political machines did not always keep their promises. For example, Tammany Hall, in New York, did improve some city services but was dishonest. One of its leaders, "Boss" William M. Tweed, bribed city leaders and cheated people out of money.

Up, Over, and Under

In the late 1800s, the development of affordable steel and the invention of the elevator made it possible to build very tall buildings, or skyscrapers. Steel helped create stronger bridges. The world's first **suspension bridge** was built in Cincinnati, Ohio, in 1866, by John Roebling, whose son and daughter-in-law later directed the building of New York's Brooklyn Bridge. In 1897 the country's first underground train system, or subway, was built in Boston, Massachusetts.

© Scott Foresman Growth of a Nation

Lesson 2: Review

1. **Cause and Effect** Complete this chart by filling in one effect of each event listed below.

Cause | **Effect**

The population grew so fast that housing couldn't keep up with it. →

Immigrants were offered help from political machines. →

Jane Addams wanted to help immigrants. →

Steel was strong enough to support great weight. →

2. How did urbanization bring about the need for settlement houses? Write two or three sentences to answer the question. Be sure to use the vocabulary words.

_____

_____

3. List three problems faced by some immigrants who moved to big cities in the late 1800s.

_____

_____

4. Why did political machines want to control the votes of immigrants?

_____

_____

5. **Critical Thinking:** *Draw Conclusions* You have read that immigrants faced many hardships in the big cities of the United States. Why do you think so many people continued to immigrate?

_____

_____

Lesson 3: Unequal Opportunities

Vocabulary

tenant a person who pays rent to use land or buildings

enfranchise to give the right to vote

Great Migration movement north from 1915–1940s of more than one million African Americans

The South After Reconstruction

After Reconstruction, the South remained the poorest section of the country. Many blacks and poor whites became **tenant** farmers. Falling crop prices and high interest rates on loans kept most sharecroppers, who paid their rent in crops, trapped in debt. Southern Democrats soon controlled all southern states and looked to the newly **enfranchised** African Americans for votes.

Prejudice and Segregation

In the 1880s, Jim Crow Laws made segregation legal in the South. In 1892 Homer Plessy, a person of mixed race, entered a whites-only section of a train in Louisiana. He was arrested. Plessy sued the state. The case went to the Supreme Court. The court found Plessy guilty and said it was legal to keep the races separate as long as facilities for whites and blacks were equal. Hispanics, Chinese, and Jews, also faced discrimination.

Great Migration

In the late 1800s and early 1900s, African Americans in the South wanted better jobs, schools, and more rights. Many believed the North might be a better place to live. Newspapers from northern cities told of homes and jobs for blacks, listing black churches and other organizations that would help when they arrived. More than one million African Americans moved north in the **Great Migration.** When northern workers left factory jobs to fight in World War I, blacks and women filled these jobs.

Life in the North

African Americans also faced discrimination in the North. Jim Crow laws kept blacks out of restaurants, hotels, and theaters. Some white property owners would not sell or rent to blacks. Blacks were crowded in certain neighborhoods, and workers were not given the same opportunities as whites. Some did find a better life in the North. Some started their own businesses. They generally earned more than blacks living in the South.

New Leaders Arise

African American leaders continued to speak out against discrimination. W. E. B. Du Bois, an African American writer and editor, helped start the National Association for the Advancement of Colored People, or NAACP, in 1909. Booker T. Washington, a former slave, founded the Tuskegee Institute in 1881, a college for African Americans in Alabama. George Washington Carver, a scientist, helped organize the school's agricultural department in 1896.

Others Join the Fight

Ida Wells-Barnett, whose parents were slaves, helped start an African American newspaper in Chicago in 1893 and defeated an Illinois law that would have segregated trains and buses.

© Scott Foresman Growth of a Nation

Lesson 3: Review

1. ⟳ **Main Idea and Details** Complete the chart below by filling in three details that support the main idea that Jim Crow laws led to segregation.

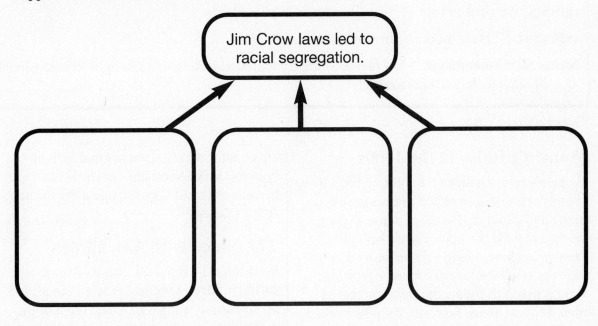

2. Why did most sharecroppers stay in debt?

_____

_____

3. What issues did African Americans face in the North?

_____

_____

4. What are some of the ways in which African American leaders responded to discrimination?

_____

_____

5. **Critical Thinking:** *Make Generalizations* Describe some of the hopes African Americans might have had when they moved North with the Great Migration. Use the highlighted term in your answer.

_____

_____

© Scott Foresman Growth of a Nation

Lesson 4: Women's Rights

Vocabulary

suffrage the right to vote

suffragist a person working for women's voting rights

Nineteenth Amendment a law added to the Constitution stating that the right to vote cannot be limited due to a person's sex

Women's Roles in the 1800s

Women's roles changed a lot during the 1800s. Women were still expected to care for the home and children. However, some women worked outside the home as teachers or factory workers. Many women worked in cities as maids or housekeepers. Few women were allowed to follow the same careers as men. In rural areas, however, couples worked together to survive. Pioneer women had fewer comforts than city women did. But they were more nearly equal to men in work and rights. New inventions for housework and farm work also changed people's lives. Many city women had more free time for visiting and shopping. As a result, the first department stores were opened. Some women who had been housekeepers found jobs in these stores.

Women Work for More Rights

In the 1800s, women could not go to college. Married women did not have the right to own property. Many women wanted to change the social and legal status of women. They wanted the same opportunities and rights as men had. Lucretia Mott and Elizabeth Cady Stanton were women's rights leaders who fought for women's education, jobs, and **suffrage.** People who worked for women's voting rights were called **suffragists.** The Fifteenth Amendment, which gave African American men the right to vote, was passed after the Civil War. Women wanted the same right. Lucy Stone, Susan B. Anthony, and Carrie Chapman Catt were leaders of the suffrage movement. Susan B. Anthony traveled the country, giving speeches and helping to organize suffrage groups. Women's suffrage became the most important goal for women's rights leaders.

The Nineteenth Amendment

World War I helped the cause of women's suffrage. Many men had entered the armed services, and women replaced them in the workforce. Women performed jobs they had never done before, such as repairing cars, driving buses, and producing weapons in factories. About 11,000 women joined the women's branch of the United States Navy. If they could do all this, women argued, they should be allowed to vote. At this time, Congress was made up entirely of men. Still, Congress passed the **Nineteenth Amendment** in 1919. It stated: "The right of citizens to vote shall not be denied or abridged [limited] by the United States or by any state on account of [the] sex [of a person]."

Other Opportunities

In the late 1800s, many colleges began to accept women students. Women began pursuing new careers. Annie Peck Smith was a university professor before she became a mountain climber. She climbed mountains all over the world. She even climbed Peru's Mount Huascaran, the tallest peak in the Western hemisphere, at the age of 60. Other women became explorers, journalists, and even spies. Opportunities for women increased in many areas.

Quick Study

Lesson 4: Review

1. ⟳ **Sequence** Redraw this chart by putting the events in their correct order.

```
┌─────────────────────────────────────┐
│  Congress approves the right to vote │
│       for all American women.        │
└─────────────────────────────────────┘
                 ↓
┌─────────────────────────────────────┐
│         African American             │
│     men get the right to vote.       │
└─────────────────────────────────────┘
                 ↓
┌─────────────────────────────────────┐
│     The Seneca Falls Convention      │
│    proposes equality for women.      │
└─────────────────────────────────────┘
                 ↓
┌─────────────────────────────────────┐
│ Susannah Medora Salter is the first woman │
│  in the United States to be elected mayor. │
└─────────────────────────────────────┘
```

2. What was the goal of the suffragists? Why did suffrage become more important to women's rights leaders after the passage of the Fifteenth Amendment?

_____

_____

3. How did Susan B. Anthony contribute to the cause of women's rights?

_____

_____

4. What rights and opportunities did women gain during the late 1800s and early 1900s?

_____

_____

5. **Critical Thinking:** *Evaluate* How do you think the work-saving tools mentioned at the beginning of this lesson, along with the way they changed people's lives, might have contributed to women having greater interest in equal rights?

_____

_____

© Scott Foresman Growth of a Nation

Lesson 1: Expanding Overseas

Vocabulary

yellow journalism false, exaggerated writing meant to sell more newspapers and influence readers

Spanish-American War war in which the United States defeated Spain in 1898 and gained Spanish territory

Rough Riders a volunteer fighting force led by Theodore Roosevelt

Buffalo Soldiers the African American soldiers who served in the war against Native Americans on the Great Plains and later served in the Spanish-American War

isthmus a narrow strip of land that connects two larger areas

Alaska

Secretary of State William Seward wanted to see the United States expand and gain valuable resources. It was his idea to buy Alaska from Russia. In 1867 the United States bought it for $7.2 million in gold. People attacked the idea, but Alaska's value was soon recognized.

Hawaii

American planters moved to Hawaii in the mid-1800s because the warm climate was perfect for sugarcane and pineapples. The Hawaiian king gave the Americans special trading rights and the use of Pearl Harbor. In 1898 Hawaii was added to the United States.

Causes of the Spanish-American War

In 1895 the Cubans revolted against Spanish rule. The United States, upset by Spain's treatment of the Cubans and afraid for its own businesses in Cuba, sent the battleship *Maine* to protect American lives and property there in 1898. An explosion destroyed the ship, killing 260 Americans. Though it may have been an accident, **yellow journalism** blamed Spain. The **Spanish-American War** began on April 25, 1898.

War with Spain

The United States Navy attacked and destroyed the Spanish fleet in the Philippines. Nearly one million Americans volunteered to fight. Theodore Roosevelt organized the **Rough Riders,** made up of cowboys, Native Americans, college athletes, and wealthy New Yorkers. The African American **Buffalo Soldiers** also went. The United States won the war quickly and in August signed a treaty with Spain.

Results of War

The United States gained control of Spanish territories including Puerto Rico, the Philippines, and Guam and became one of the most powerful nations in the world.

Panama Canal

U.S. ships wanted to travel faster between the Atlantic and Pacific Oceans. Backed by the United States, Panama declared independence from Colombia in 1903 and let the United States build a canal across the **Isthmus** of Panama. Dr. Walter Reed discovered that mosquitoes carried diseases like yellow fever and malaria. Dr. W.C. Gorgas drained areas where mosquitoes laid eggs. On August 15, 1914, the 50-mile canal opened.

Panama Today

A 1977 treaty with the United States gave Panama full control of the canal in 2000.

© Scott Foresman Growth of a Nation

Lesson 1: Review

1. **Cause and Effect** Complete the chart by filling in an effect of each major event from this lesson.

Cause	Effect
Gold was discovered in Alaska. →	
The *Maine* exploded in a Cuban harbor. →	
The United States wanted a quick route from one coast to the other. →	
W.C. Gorgas worked to drain standing water in Panama. →	

2. Why did William Seward want to buy Alaska?

_____

_____

3. Why did American planters move to Hawaii?

_____

_____

4. How did yellow journalism help bring about the Spanish-American War? Answer in two or more sentences. Use the highlighted terms.

_____

_____

5. **Critical Thinking:** *Draw Conclusions* By 1900 the United States was seen as a world power. How do you think the events described in this lesson helped the United States become a world power?

_____

_____

Lesson 2: The Progressive Movement

Vocabulary

trust a group that can control a whole industry by driving out competition

Progressives reformers who wanted to stop the unfair practices by businesses and improve the way government worked

muckraker a writer who uncovered terrible working and living conditions

Blue Laws laws designed to solve some of the social problems of the early 1900s

conservation protecting something from being destroyed or used up

Problems of an Industrial Society

As industry grew in the United States, it created problems. Factories could be dangerous, unhealthy places. Some industries filled the air with smoke. Others dumped waste into rivers or lakes and cut down forests. There were frequent explosions and accidents in coal mines. Companies joined to form **trusts** to control whole industries and drive out competition. When companies compete with each other, the result is better products and lower prices. Without competition, trusts could charge higher prices for their products.

Theodore Roosevelt and the Progressives

Theodore Roosevelt was Vice-President under President McKinley. When McKinley was assassinated, Roosevelt became President. He was elected for a full term in 1904. Roosevelt agreed with the goals of the **Progressives.** One group of Progressives was made up of writers called **muckrakers.** Ida Tarbell wrote about how trusts hurt companies. In 1902 she wrote a series of articles about how Standard Oil controlled the oil industry. Roosevelt used the 1890 Sherman Antitrust Act to force trusts to break up. In 1906 Upton Sinclair's novel *The Jungle* told of unhealthy conditions in Chicago meatpacking plants. Because of this book, Roosevelt signed The Meat Inspection Act and the Pure Food and Drug Act.

Progressives also tried to improve education, health, and social problems.

Impact of Reforms

Progressives helped many new laws, such as building codes that made tenements, factories, and coal mines safer. Young children could not work in factories and had to go to school. **Blue Laws** were passed in many towns. One law meant to solve alcohol abuse said people could not buy alcohol on Sundays. Some people did not like the government forcing its morals on them. Progressives introduced the income tax in 1913 to raise money to pay for reforms and other projects.

Caring for Nature

Progressives and others cared about saving the wilderness. Yellowstone National Park became the world's first national park in 1872. John Muir, a naturalist and writer, had a great impact on the **conservation** of the country's most beautiful areas. He helped establish Yosemite National Park in California in 1890 and the Sierra Club in 1892. Theodore Roosevelt created the National Wildlife Refuge Program and the U.S. Forestry Service. He created 16 national monuments, 51 wildlife refuges, and 5 new national parks.

Lesson 2: Review

1. ↻ **Compare and Contrast** Pick three or four problems that the Progressives tried to solve. Complete this diagram by comparing life before Progressives tried to solve the problems with life after they acted.

Before

After

2. What were the Blue Laws? Why did some people not like them?

_____

_____

3. Why did Progressives want to see trusts broken up?

_____

_____

4. Describe some of the work that John Muir did to promote conservation. Use the highlighted terms in your answer.

_____

_____

5. **Critical Thinking:** *Draw Conclusions* Why do you think writers such as Ida Tarbell and Upton Sinclair were so important to the Progressive Movement?

_____

_____

Lesson 3: World War I

Vocabulary

World War I a war fought from 1914–1918, mainly involving countries of Europe and the United States

nationalism a love of one's country and a desire to keep others from controlling it

alliance an agreement among nations to defend one another

isolationism a policy to not get involved in the affairs of other countries

League of Nations an international organization formed to prevent wars

Treaty of Versailles the treaty that officially ended World War I

Gathering Storm

There were many reasons for **World War I.** Among European nations, there were strong military rivalries and feelings of **nationalism.** European countries formed **alliances.** The two major alliances were the Allied Powers (Great Britain, France, Russia, Serbia, and Belgium) and the Central Powers (Germany, Austria-Hungary, Bulgaria, and Turkey). On June 24, 1914, a Serbian nationalist assassinated Archduke Franz Ferdinand of Austria-Hungary. Austria-Hungary declared war on Serbia.

Fighting Begins in Europe

By the summer of 1914, every major country in Europe was in the war. The fighting was fierce, and it seemed the killing would never end.

The United States Enters the War

At first, the United States stayed out of the war because of its policy of **isolationism.** In 1915, a German submarine sank the British steamship, *Lusitania,* killing more than 100 U.S. citizens. Early in 1917, the United States learned that Germany was trying to get Mexico to enter the war on its side. Germany also sank three American-owned trade ships. President Woodrow Wilson asked Congress to declare war on the Central Powers.

America at War

American forces fighting in Europe was one of the deciding factors in the Allied Powers' victory.

New Technologies

Poison gas, airplanes, tanks, and machine guns were introduced as weapons, and submarines were used on a large scale.

War's Impact at Home

With fewer farmers at home to work the farms, less food was produced, so people started raising vegetables in "war gardens." More women and African Americans worked in factories.

The War Ends

The Central Powers surrendered on November 11, 1918. Millions of people had died.

The United States and the Peace Process

In 1919 President Wilson and other Allied leaders drew up the **Treaty of Versailles.** It included Wilson's idea of the **League of Nations.** The United States did not approve the treaty or join the League, thus returning to isolationism.

© Scott Foresman Growth of a Nation

Lesson 3: Review

1.  **Compare and Contrast** Complete the chart by filling in the boxes to describe what life was like in the United States before and during World War I.

Before World War I   **During World War I**

2. Identify the two alliances that fought each other in World War I and the nations that belonged to each. Answer in one or two sentences. Use the highlighted terms.

_____

_____

3. Why did the United States have a policy of isolationism, and what happened to change the policy?

_____

_____

4. Describe new technologies that were developed and used during World War I and how these technologies affected the way people fought.

_____

_____

5. **Critical Thinking:** *Draw Conclusions* Why did so many people at home get involved in the effort to help win the war?

_____

_____

Lesson 1: An Industrial Nation

Vocabulary

assembly line a line of factory workers who stand in one place and put together parts that pass by on a moving belt

mass production the making of large numbers of the same item

mass media public forms of communication that reach large audiences

Ford's Model T

Henry Ford built the Model T car in 1908. It was manufactured until 1927. The invention had a great effect on American life. Model Ts were exactly alike. They were built on an **assembly line.** Each car could be built in an hour and a half instead of 12 hours. Ford sold them for $500, less than half the cost of other cars. He paid his workers over twice as much as most other car factory workers. Ford built the first assembly line factory in Detroit, Michigan. By 1913 Model Ts made up 40 percent of the cars sold in the U.S. In 1920 half the cars in the world were Model Ts.

A Nation of Drivers

By 1929 there were about 26 million cars in the United States. Cars changed the nation. There was a demand for better roads. Governments raised money for improvements through taxes and traffic tickets. New jobs were created in car factories, road construction, and auto repair. Hotels, gas stations, and restaurants opened to serve travelers. People could live farther from their jobs and many moved out of the cities.

The Age of Radio

Mass production spread to many different industries. The radio became one of the most popular mass-produced items. The first radio message was sent across the Atlantic in 1901 by Gugielmo Marconi. He then sold radios for communication between ships. In 1916 one of his employees, David Sarnoff, suggested he sell radios to people for home entertainment.

Marconi's company rejected the idea. Frank Conrad, an engineer at Westinghouse Electric, started the first professional radio station in 1920. It was KDKA, in Pittsburgh, Pennsylvania. The first broadcast was the results of the Presidential race between Warren Harding and James Cox. Meanwhile, Sarnoff presented his ideas to a new company, the Radio Corporation of America (RCA). RCA made radios for home use. Radio sales soared after RCA broadcast a 1921 championship boxing match. Comedy, music, and drama programs were created.

Mass Media

At first broadcasting was a way to sell radios. Radio companies then began making money by selling airtime to companies to advertise their products. Commercials were born. Radio joined newspapers as a form of **mass media.** Families around the country sat down to listen to favorite shows, songs became popular, mass media began to shape a common American culture.

Going to the Movies

Short silent movies became popular in the early 1900s. Hollywood, California, became the center of the movie industry. Movies also shaped American culture. Moviegoers often copied the hairstyles and clothes of movie stars. By 1920 35 million people went to the movies every week. In 1927 movies added sound.

Lesson 1: Review

1. 🔄 **Draw Conclusions** Complete the chart by filling in a conclusion supported by the facts given.

Facts

The automobile made long-distance travel easier than before.

People listening to radio bought many of the same products.

Moviegoers often copied the hairstyles and clothes of movie stars.

Conclusion

2. What effect did Henry Ford's assembly line bring to American industry?

_____

_____

3. List some of the major events that led to the Age of Radio.

_____

_____

4. How did mass media affect business and audiences?

_____

_____

5. **Critical Thinking:** *Compare and Contrast* Compare and contrast the effects of the new technologies on life in the country.

_____

_____

Lesson 2: The Roaring Twenties

Vocabulary

Prohibition a legal ban on the sale of alcohol

Eighteenth Amendment a law added to the Constitution outlawing the manufacture, sale, and transport of alcohol

Twenty-first Amendment a law added to the Constitution that ended Prohibition

jazz a form of music that grew out of African American traditions

Harlem Renaissance a period of achievement in music, art, and writing by African Americans living in Harlem

Prohibition

Reformers, concerned that people abused alcohol, called for **Prohibition.** The **Eighteenth Amendment** to the Constitution was passed in 1919. Alcohol abuse declined, but many felt the government should not control people's behavior. Bootleggers made and smuggled alcohol. Then they sold it to speakeasies, illegal places where people drank. Police could not stop the bootleggers. In 1933 the **Twenty-first Amendment** was passed.

The Jazz Age

In the 1920s, radio and movies helped **jazz** become popular. Duke Ellington was a famous jazz composer and bandleader. Louis Armstrong was an important jazz trumpet player, songwriter, and singer. New dances spread around the nation, like the Charleston and the Lindy Hop.

Changing Culture

Jazz influenced all the arts in the 1920s. Artists such as writer F. Scott Fitzgerald, composers George Gershwin and Aaron Copland, and dancers Isadora Duncan and Martha Graham reflected the new spirit of the times in their work.

The Harlem Renaissance

In the 1920s, many African American artists moved to the neighborhood of Harlem in New York City. This period is called the **Harlem Renaissance.** Writers such as James Weldon Johnson, Langston Hughes, and Zora Neale Hurston wrote about the lives of African Americans and how they had been treated unfairly. Jacob Lawrence created paintings about African American life and history.

Athletes and Pilots

News of sports events and historic accomplishments in the 1920s spread quickly through the mass media such as radio and newspapers. Gertrude Ederle was the first woman to swim across the English Channel. Baseball player Babe Ruth hit 60 home runs in one season. Pilot Charles Lindbergh, known as "Lucky Lindy," became the first person to fly alone across the Atlantic Ocean in 1927. In the early 1930s, Amelia Earhart became the first woman to fly across the Atlantic alone.

Women at Work

Women got the right to vote in 1920 and could work in offices instead of factories. Some, such as Amelia Earhart and painter Georgia O'Keeffe, became leaders in their fields.

© Scott Foresman Growth of a Nation

Lesson 2: Review

1. ⟳ **Draw Conclusions** Complete the chart by filling in the missing facts that lead to the given conclusion.

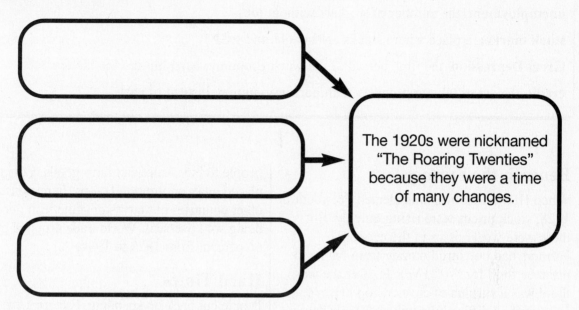

The 1920s were nicknamed "The Roaring Twenties" because they were a time of many changes.

2. What led to the adoption of the Eighteenth and Twenty-first Amendments?

_____

_____

3. What was the purpose of the work of Harlem Renaissance artists?

_____

_____

4. How did the mass media help make athletes and pilots famous?

_____

_____

5. **Critical Thinking:** *Analyze* What changes occurred for working women in the 1920s?

_____

_____

Lesson 3: The Good Times End

Vocabulary

unemployment the number of workers without jobs

stock market a place where stocks are bought and sold

Great Depression the time period of the worst economic hardship in U.S. history

credit the act of buying products with borrowed money instead of cash

Beneath the Surface

When Herbert Hoover was elected President in 1928, stock prices were rising quickly. But there were weaknesses in the economy. Farmers had borrowed money from banks to produce food for World War I. After the war, there was a surplus of crops. Crop prices fell. Farmers had difficulty paying off their debts. Factories were producing more goods than they could sell. Many began to lay off workers in the late 1920s. **Unemployment** began to rise. Industries such as mining and lumber lost customers who switched to other products.

The Stock Market Crash

Companies sell shares, called stocks, to investors on the **stock market.** Stock prices rose steadily in the 1920s. In October 1929, the market crashed. Prices fell quickly, causing many investors to panic and sell their stocks. By November, investors had lost $26 billion. Many people lost all of their money.

Causes of the Depression

The country entered the **Great Depression.** Many investors had bought stocks on **credit.** After the crash, people owed more money than their stocks were worth. Customers rushed the banks to withdraw all of their money. By 1933, 11,000 out of 25,000 banks had closed. People lost their entire savings. Then, to encourage people to buy American farm goods, Congress placed a tax on imported crops. In response, other countries put tariffs on American goods being sold overseas. World trade dropped by 66 percent from 1929 to 1934.

Hard Times

People cut back on spending. Factories cut production or closed. By 1932 about 25 percent of the workers were unemployed. Many people lost their homes and faced poverty. Less income meant less income tax money for governments and schools. Teachers' pay was cut, and some schools closed. Crop prices continued to fall. President Hoover asked business leaders not to lay off workers. He urged local government to create jobs by constructing roads and buildings.

Surviving the Depression

High school and college graduates could not find jobs. Many people delayed marriage. Families struggled. Women and children worked. People stood in breadlines and built shantytowns made of cardboard or cheap wood.

The Election of 1932

By 1932 people felt that Hoover's government should do more. Franklin D. Roosevelt was elected president because citizens believed he would help change things.

© Scott Foresman Growth of a Nation

Lesson 3: Review

1. ⟳ **Cause and Effect** Complete the chart below by filling in the effects of each cause of the Great Depression.

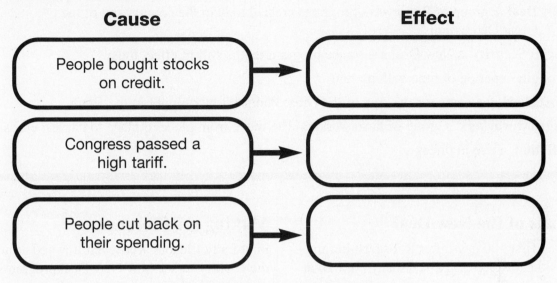

Cause		Effect

People bought stocks on credit. →

Congress passed a high tariff. →

People cut back on their spending. →

2. What were some weaknesses in the economy of the 1920s?

_____

_____

3. What were the main events of the stock market crash?

_____

_____

_____

4. What were some causes of the Great Depression?

_____

_____

_____

5. **Critical Thinking:** *Cause and Effect* How did the Great Depression change the lives of Americans?

_____

_____

_____

_____

Name _____   Date _____

Lesson 4: The New Deal

Vocabulary

New Deal a group of Roosevelt's programs created to help the country out of the Great Depression

Social Security a New Deal assistance program that is still in effect today

drought a period of time with no rain

Dust Bowl the name for the area of the Great Plains hit by drought in the 1930s

migrant workers a group of farm workers who move from place to place to harvest crops

inflation a rise in prices

Goals of the New Deal

In the first 100 days after Roosevelt became President, Congress passed many **New Deal** programs. The goals of the New Deal were relief, recovery, and reform. Relief programs helped people. Recovery programs stimulated the economy. Reform programs tried to prevent the Depression from occurring again. One $500 million relief program fed and housed the poorest people in the country. Another program for recovery helped farmers to buy equipment. In addition, the Securities and Exchange Commission (SEC) was created to protect stock market investors. The programs helped people survive, but the Great Depression continued through the 1930s. Some of the New Deal programs, like **Social Security,** are still in effect today. The reforms gave the federal government a bigger role in people's lives.

The Dust Bowl

A **drought** hit the Great Plains in the mid-1930s. Soil turned to dust and scattered in high winds called dust storms. The region became known as the **Dust Bowl.** Over three million people left their farms. They moved west to work in California as **migrant workers.** But many were unable to find jobs.

Making a Difference

First Lady Eleanor Roosevelt traveled around the country to see how New Deal programs were working. She wanted to make sure that women, children, and African Americans were being treated fairly. Dorothea Lange, a photographer hired by the Farm Security Agency, showed the effects of the Great Depression in her famous photographs of migrant workers. In 1939 John Steinbeck published *The Grapes of Wrath*, a novel about a migrant family in the Dust Bowl.

Entertainment During Hard Times

The Great Depression was still not over in 1939, despite the New Deal programs. People looked for ways to forget their troubles without spending a lot of money. Comic books were created with characters like Superman and Batman. People played board games like *Monopoly®*. Drive-in movie theaters were built. Movies made more money than ever before. Millions of people attended the World's Fair held in Queens, New York, to see technology and art from 60 countries.

Global Depression

Millions of people around the world struggled through the Great Depression. Germany had huge debts after losing World War I. **Inflation** soared, and German money became worthless.

© Scott Foresman Growth of a Nation

Lesson 4: Review

1. ⊙ **Main Idea and Details** Complete the graphic organizer to show details supporting the main idea. (See p. 330 in your textbook.)

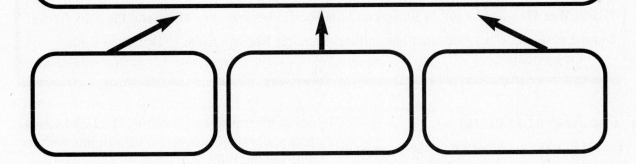

New Deal programs were an "alphabet soup" of government agencies that tried to help people during the Great Depression.

2. What caused the Dust Bowl? How did it affect farmers of the Great Plains?

   _____

   _____

3. How did artists such as Dorothea Lange and John Steinbeck make people aware of the hardships of the Great Depression?

   _____

   _____

4. Why were forms of entertainment such as movies and board games popular in the 1930s?

   _____

   _____

5. **Critical Thinking:** *Draw Conclusions* Why do you think the Great Depression spread around the world?

   _____

   _____

Name ＿＿＿＿＿＿＿＿＿＿ Date ＿＿＿＿＿

Lesson 1: World War II Begins

Vocabulary

dictator a leader with absolute power over the nation's government

fascism a form of government that denies individual freedom and gives complete control to the government

Axis the allied military dictatorships of Germany, Italy, and Japan

Allies the countries that united to fight the Axis during World War II

World War II a war fought in Europe and the Pacific between the Allies and the Axis forces

Lend-Lease the U.S. policy that lent military supplies free of charge to Britain to fight the Germans

The Rise of Dictators

People in some countries hit by the depression were desperate for change. **Dictators** came into power. Adolf Hitler became the dictator of Germany in 1933. His party, the Nazis, believed in **fascism.** Hitler believed that Germans were superior to other people. His speeches attacked Jewish people and promised to expand Germany's borders. Benito Mussolini, another dictator, took power in Italy in the 1920s and wanted to conquer other countries. In Japan, a small group of military leaders came to power, seeking to build an empire in East Asia.

The Axis Powers

In the mid-1930s, the **Axis** struck. Italy invaded and colonized Ethiopia. Japan invaded China. Germany took control of Austria and Czechoslovakia. In 1939 Hitler invaded Poland, and the **Allies** declared war on Germany. **World War II** had begun. The German military defeated Poland, then moved west to conquer most of Western Europe. France fell to Germany in 1940, leaving Britain to fight alone.

The Debate at Home

Germany continuously bombed British cities in 1940. Winston Churchill, Britain's leader, asked Roosevelt for help. Because of the Great Depression and World War I, many Americans supported the idea of isolationism, or staying

out of other nations' problems. The **Lend-Lease** policy allowed Roosevelt to help Britain without entering the fight.

Declaring War

In 1941 the British beat Germany in the Battle of Britain. But Japan controlled much of China and Southeast Asia. U.S. leaders opposed Japanese expansion. Japan bombed the U.S. naval base at Pearl Harbor in Hawaii on December 7, 1941, killing more than 2,300 people. The United States quickly declared war on Japan. Germany and Italy declared war on the United States, which now became one of the Allies.

Axis Advances

When the United States entered World War II, the Axis controlled most of Europe, North Africa, and East Asia. Months earlier, Hitler had broken an agreement with Soviet dictator Joseph Stalin and invaded the Soviet Union, which joined the Allies. The United States, once enemies with the Soviet Union, sent them military supplies and food under the Lend-Lease program.

The Draft

As the U. S. entered World War II, it was not prepared to fight a major war. The government had to draft 10 million men into the military.

© Scott Foresman Growth of a Nation

Lesson 1: Review

1. ⟳ **Draw Conclusions** Complete the chart by filling in a conclusion that could be drawn from the facts given below.

By 1942 Germany had conquered most of Europe.

By 1942 Japan had built a huge empire in East Asia.

2. What actions by Adolf Hitler led to the start of World War II?

_____

_____

_____

3. How did Japan's attack on Pearl Harbor affect feelings of isolationism in the United States?

_____

_____

_____

4. List the major powers of the Axis and the Allies.

_____

_____

_____

5. **Critical Thinking:** *Express Ideas* Do you think it took courage for President Roosevelt to decide to lend Britain supplies?

_____

_____

_____

Lesson 2: The Home Front

Vocabulary

rationing the practice of limiting the amount of food people can buy

Tuskegee Airmen a unit of African American fighter pilots trained in Tuskegee, Alabama

atomic bomb a bomb that releases a massive explosion by splitting atoms

Manhattan Project the name for the U.S. project to build the first atomic bomb

The Depression Ends

American industry used its resources to build military equipment. Automobile companies stopped making cars to make military tanks and trucks. Shipyards operated 24 hours a day. By 1945 the U.S. airplane industry was the biggest industry in the world. This created millions of new jobs. The Great Depression finally ended. Industrial cities grew as America poured its energy into working for the Allied war effort.

New Jobs for Women

350,000 women served in World War II. Women like Gertrude Pearson who worked close to combat helped change attitudes towards women. Women served as nurses, pilots, radio operators, and mechanics. Because of a shortage of male workers at home, by 1944 3.5 million women were working in weapons factories.

"Do Your Part"

Posters and commercials told Americans to "Do Your Part." Children organized "scrap drives" for metal, to fight shortages. With millions of soldiers to feed, the government used **rationing.** Families also planted "Victory Gardens" for food.

New Opportunities

Labor shortages gave African Americans new job opportunities. But workers received lower wages than white workers and soldiers served in segregated units. The Air Corps did not accept black pilots. African American leaders protested this policy, and thirteen of them formed the **Tuskegee Airmen.** Their commander Benjamin O. Davis became the first African American General in the U.S. Air Force. Over one million African Americans served in the military. By the end of the war, some served in integrated units.

Japanese Americans

In 1941 there were about 125,000 Japanese Americans living in the United States. Fearing that the Japanese Americans living on the West Coast would help Japan, Roosevelt ordered the military to force more than 110,000 Japanese Americans from their homes and into internment camps. Still, thousands of Japanese Americans served in the U.S. military.

Technology and War

Axis and Allied countries competed to invent new weapons. The scientist Albert Einstein warned Roosevelt that Germany might be working on an **atomic bomb.** In 1942 the U.S. government started the **Manhattan Project.** In 1945 they tested the first atomic bomb in Los Alamos, New Mexico. Scientists also developed secret codes, computers to break codes, and radar to detect enemies at night.

© Scott Foresman Growth of a Nation

Lesson 2: Review

1. ⟳ **Main Idea and Details** Complete this chart by filling in details that support the main idea.

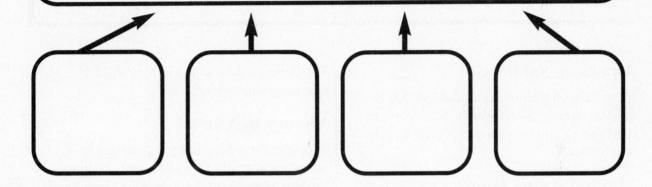

During World War II, many people in the United States found new opportunities and faced new challenges.

2. How did World War II affect the United States economy?

_____

_____

3. How did children contribute to the war effort in the United States and Britain?

_____

_____

4. What was the goal of the Manhattan Project?

_____

_____

5. **Critical Thinking:** *Decision Making* Do you think the military draft was a good idea? Explain your answer.

_____

_____

Lesson 3: The World at War

Vocabulary

Battle of Midway the turning point in the war against Japan

Battle of Stalingrad the turning point in the war against Germany

Battle of the Bulge the last attack by the Germans

concentration camps slave labor camps where Jews were detained or killed

Holocaust the systematic widespread killing of the Jews and others by Nazis

American Soldiers

More than 16 million Americans served in the military during World War II. Navajo soldiers used their language as a secret code to help win battles.

Major Turning Points

In 1942 the **Battle of Midway** was a turning point in the war against Japan. After destroying many of the U.S. Navy's ships at Pearl Harbor, the Japanese hoped to destroy more ships at Midway Island. But U.S. code-breakers told Admiral Chester Nimitz where the attack would take place. American navy pilots destroyed many Japanese ships and planes. The Japanese fleet became too weak to capture more Pacific islands. The United States began to win back territory. The **Battle of Stalingrad** was a turning point in the war against Germany. After their victory in this battle in early 1943, Soviet armies began forcing the Germans to retreat.

Victory in Europe

In 1944 Western Europe was still controlled by the Germans. U.S. General Dwight D. Eisenhower conducted the largest invasion by sea in world history. On the morning of June 6, 1944, known as "D-Day," American, British, and Canadian soldiers landed in German-controlled France. In December 1944 Germany attacked in the **Battle of the Bulge.**

The Allied forces won. On May 8, 1945, Germany surrendered.

Victory in Asia

Fighting toward Japan by capturing key islands was costly for U.S. troops. Military leaders were afraid that invading Japan would cost one million American lives. President Roosevelt died in April 1945, and Vice-President Harry Truman became president. Later, he decided to use newly tested atomic bombs. The first of two bombs was dropped on Hiroshima, killing over 80,000 people in a few seconds. Japan surrendered on August 14, 1945.

The Holocaust

Hitler's Nazi party had a policy of anti-Semitism, or hatred of Jewish people. The Nazis tried to eliminate the entire Jewish population in Europe. They captured Jews in each country they conquered and sent them to **concentration camps.** Many were murdered. Others worked as slave laborers and died of hunger or disease. After the war, Allied soldiers were shocked to discover the camps. In the **Holocaust,** the Nazis had murdered 6 million Jews and 6 million non-Jews.

The Costs of War

Between 40 and 50 million people died during World War II. The world now faced the threat of a new weapon, the atomic bomb.

© Scott Foresman Growth of a Nation

Lesson 3: Review

1. 🔄 **Sequence** Complete the chart by filling in major events that led to the end of World War II. Include the month and year of each event.

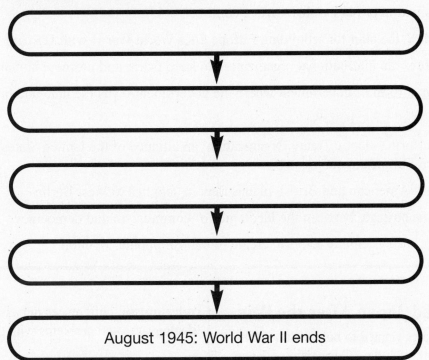

2. Identify one major turning point in World War II and explain its importance.

_____

_____

_____

3. What effect did the use of atomic bombs have on the outcome of World War II?

_____

_____

4. Summarize the events of the Holocaust.

_____

_____

5. **Critical Thinking: *Analyze Primary Sources*** You read that when Truman became President he said, "I felt like the moon, the stars, and all the planets had fallen on me." What do you think he meant by this? (See p. 361 of your textbook.)

_____

_____

Lesson 1: The World is Divided

Vocabulary

aggressor a nation or person that starts a conflict

Marshall Plan the plan for rebuilding Europe after World War II with U.S. aid

United Nations an international organization to keep peace and promote human rights

communism a form of government where the government owns the land and businesses

ideology a set of basic beliefs

NATO The North Atlantic Treaty Organization; an alliance of the United States, Canada, and Western European countries

Berlin Airlift American and British planes flew in supplies to West Berlin

Cold War the struggle between the ideologies of communism and democracy

propaganda the systematic effort to create or control popular opinion

Europe and Japan After the War

The United Sates wanted to help the countries hurt by the war, including Germany and Japan, even though they had been the **aggressors.** Japan adopted a democratic form of government. Stalin, Roosevelt, and Churchill decided how to rebuild Europe. Stalin took control over countries that bordered the Soviet Union. The Allied forces remained in Europe to keep peace. Korea was divided by the two superpowers, the United States and the Soviet Union.

Continuing Aid

Secretary of State George C. Marshall's plan for rebuilding Europe, the **Marshall Plan,** gave over $13 billion in U.S. aid. This assistance promoted democratic governments.

The United Nations

Representatives from 50 different countries formed the **United Nations** in 1945 to promote global cooperation. President Roosevelt was one of the main designers. His wife, Eleanor, helped write the Universal Declaration of Human Rights.

Troubling Differences

The Soviet Union's government was based on communism. Differences in basic beliefs, or **ideology,** created problems with the West.

The Iron Curtain Falls

The Soviet Union controlled countries east of the so-called Iron Curtain. The United States and other countries formed **NATO** in 1949, to guard against the Soviet Union.

The Berlin Airlift

Stalin cut off supplies to West Berlin in 1948, but the **Berlin Airlift** saved the city.

A New Kind of War

The Soviets backed communist governments in Europe, China, and North Korea. The United States supported democracies and free enterprise. This struggle became known as the **Cold War.** Neither country attacked the other, but they competed for power and influence around the world. Both sides used **propaganda.**

A World Divided

As the world began to split between the Free World and the Communist World, the Soviet Union focused on controlling developing countries. The Free World wanted to stop the growth of communism.

Lesson 1: Review

1. ↻ **Cause and Effect** Complete this chart by filling in one cause for each effect listed below.

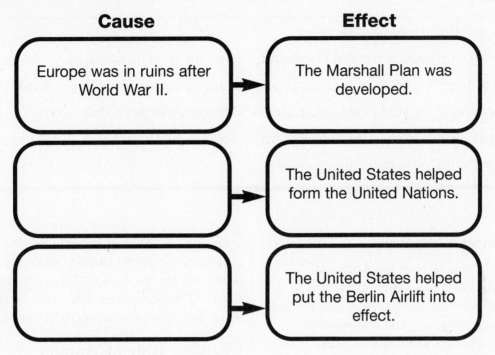

Cause   **Effect**

Europe was in ruins after World War II. → The Marshall Plan was developed.

→ The United States helped form the United Nations.

→ The United States helped put the Berlin Airlift into effect.

2. Describe the conditions Europe and Asia faced following World War II.

_____

_____

3. How did the ideologies of the United States and the Soviet Union bring about the Cold War between the Soviet Union and the United States? Write two or more sentences to answer the question. Be sure to use the highlighted words in your answer.

_____

_____

4. **Critical Thinking: *Draw Conclusions*** In what ways might the Marshall Plan help stop the spread of communism?

_____

_____

5. What role did the United States play in the development of the United Nations?

_____

_____

Lesson 2: Boom Years at Home

Vocabulary

suburbs residential areas outside cities

AFL-CIO labor organization that represented 85 percent of union members

G.I. Bill of Rights a group of benefits given to returning soldiers from World War II

consumer credit the credit used by consumers who borrow money to buy goods

credit card a card for charging consumer purchases that can be paid back in installments

commute the daily trip from home to work

A Growing Economy

After World War II, reunited American families felt optimistic about the future. Rationing was over. Cars, televisions, portable radios, barbecue grills, and toys were in demand. Industries expanded to meet consumer demand. New jobs offered good wages and benefits. **Suburbs** were created as builders bought up land outside cities.

The Changing Workplace

Veterans returned to the workplace, and many working women returned to the home. Labor unions had become strong. The average workweek had decreased from 59 hours in 1900 to 40.5 hours in 1950. Unions became more powerful in the 1950s as the numbers of workers grew. In 1955, the American Federation of Labor and the Congress of Industrial Organizations merged into the **AFL-CIO,** bringing together 85 percent of all union members.

The G.I. Bill

The **G.I. Bill of Rights** offered returning veterans education and training, home and business loans, unemployment pay, and job placement assistance.

The Rise of Credit Society

Millions of veterans took advantage of government loans. Soon the loans were extended to civilians. **Consumer credit** was born. People could now use **credit cards** to buy consumer goods and pay for them by the month. From 1950 to 1960, consumer debt in the United States rose from $73 billion to $196 billion.

Evolving Role of Women

By 1960, 36 percent of American women worked outside the home. Improved appliances and public kindergarten gave women more free time. Professional women were usually paid less than men. Eleanor Roosevelt advocated for women's rights.

Changing Life

From 1950 to 1960, the number of children in the United States under 18 increased from 47.3 million to 64.2 million. Parents who had lived through the Great Depression and who had used the G.I. Bill saw education as the key to prosperity. Inner city schools suffered as people and their tax money moved to the suburbs. New highways were crowded with people who **commuted,** or drove, to work.

The Technology Explosion

Technologies developed that helped Americans. Commercial air travel began. Entertainment became an important industry. Direct dial telephone service became available in 1952. Computers the size of a room aided in developing more technology.

© Scott Foresman Growth of a Nation

Lesson 2: Review

1. ⊙ **Cause and Effect** Complete this chart by filling in the missing effects of the major events from this lesson.

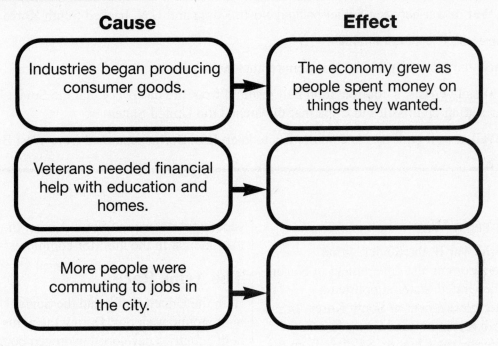

Cause

Effect

Industries began producing consumer goods. → The economy grew as people spent money on things they wanted.

Veterans needed financial help with education and homes. →

More people were commuting to jobs in the city. →

2. What is consumer credit?

_____

_____

3. Describe how the G.I. Bill helped returning war veterans. Answer in two or more sentences. Use the highlighted term in your answer.

_____

_____

4. In your own words, summarize the positive changes many American families experienced in the 1950s. Answer in two or more sentences.

_____

_____

5. **Critical Thinking:** *Evaluate* Which 1950s technology—television, air conditioning, or interstate highways—do you think has the biggest impact on your life today? Explain your answer.

_____

_____

© Scott Foresman Growth of a Nation

Lesson 3: Cold War Conflicts

Vocabulary

Korean War a war between Soviet-backed North Korea and U.N.-backed South Korea

Red Scare the fear of communism

arms race the race to build better and more nuclear weapons

Cuban Missile Crisis a confrontation that resulted from the discovery that the Soviet Union was setting up missiles in Cuba that threatened the United States

Berlin Wall a wall built by the communists to keep East Berlin separated from West Berlin

The Korean War

After World War II, the Soviet Union supported a communist government in North Korea. The United States supported a democratic government in South Korea. In 1950 North Korea invaded South Korea, helped later by the Chinese. Soldiers from the United States and 15 other countries drove the communists back. President Truman did not want another country controlled by the Soviets. The **Korean War** ended in 1953, and more than 33,000 American soldiers died.

Divided Korea

Korea stayed divided and U.S. soldiers remained there to prevent another invasion.

Continuing Tensions

The United States and other Free nations feared communism would spread in Southeast Asia, so they made an alliance called the South East Asia Treaty Organization, or SEATO.

The Red Scare at Home

By 1919, the American Communist Party had 70,000 members. The **Red Scare** referred to concerns about a communist revolution. In 1950 Senator Joseph McCarthy warned the public that there were communists in the government, and many innocent people lost their jobs because of accusations. After the

successful defense of South Korea, the public lost interest in the hunt for communists.

The Arms Race

Both the United States and the Soviet Union built atomic weapons. During the **arms race,** both countries developed hydrogen bombs that were 1,000 times more powerful than atomic bombs. Americans built underground shelters in case of a nuclear attack. The government felt that the only way to prevent a Soviet attack was to stay ahead in the arms race.

The Cuban Missile Crisis

Supported by the Soviet Union, Fidel Castro established a communist government in Cuba. In 1962 U.S. planes spied the Soviets setting up nuclear missiles in Cuba, 90 miles from Florida. President John F. Kennedy sent the U.S. Navy to block Soviet ships bringing more missiles. During the **Cuban Missile Crisis,** people feared a nuclear war. Finally, the Soviets agreed to remove the missiles from Cuba.

The Arms Race Continues

Kennedy wanted to avoid further crises, but the communist threat was still strong. The **Berlin Wall** was erected in 1961 to keep people in communist East Berlin from fleeing to West Berlin. People who tried to escape were shot.

© Scott Foresman Growth of a Nation

Lesson 3: Review

1. ⟳ **Summarize** Complete the chart by summarizing the results in the United States Cold War conflicts. Answer in a complete sentence or two.

Events

| The Korean War | The Cuban Missile Crisis | The Red Scare |

2. Why did Truman believe the United States should fight in the Korean War?

_____

_____

3. Describe Senator Joseph McCarthy's role in the Red Scare of the 1950s. Answer in one or more complete sentences. Use the highlighted terms in your answer.

_____

_____

_____

4. What actions did Kennedy take after Soviet missiles were discovered in Cuba? Answer in two or more complete sentences.

_____

_____

_____

5. **Critical Thinking: *Express Ideas*** Do you believe it was important for the United States to stay ahead of the Soviet Union in the arms race? Explain.

_____

_____

Lesson 1: African Americans and Civil Rights

Vocabulary

civil rights rights guaranteed to all United States citizens by the Constitution

passive resistance protest through nonviolent means

Segregation

African American culture flourished across the United States, despite hardship. African Americans had separate businesses, churches, schools, and colleges. By the mid-1900s, black entertainers had gained fortune and recognition around the world. As African Americans became more educated and successful, the problem of social isolation and the need for equality became more evident.

The Struggle Continues

African American individuals such as Bessie Coleman, Richard Wright, Jackie Robinson, and Benjamin O. Davis earned fame and admiration for their work, despite discrimination. After the war, many people joined the struggle for **civil rights.**

Ending School Segregation

Schools for African American children often received much less funding than schools for white children. The head lawyer of the NAACP, Thurgood Marshall, wanted to end segregation. He represented Linda Brown in the 1954 case of *Brown* v. *Board of Education.* The Supreme Court ruled that segregation of public schools was unconstitutional.

The Montgomery Bus Boycott

Under state law in Montgomery, Alabama, African Americans on a bus had to sit in the back and give up their seats to white passengers. In 1955 Rosa Parks refused to give up her seat, and she was arrested. African American leaders organized a bus boycott. In 1956 the Supreme Court ruled that segregation on public buses was illegal.

The Movement Grows

Martin Luther King, Jr., promoted the idea of **passive resistance.** In 1960 four black students in North Carolina sat at a lunch counter, for whites only, until the restaurant closed. Similar sit-ins happened around the country. African Americans and many whites took "freedom rides" on public transportation to test the new laws prohibiting segregation. Marches were held to support civil rights.

Gains and Losses

In 1963 over 200,000 Americans marched in Washington, D.C., to support President Kennedy's proposed Civil Rights Act. After Kennedy was assassinated in 1963, President Lyndon Johnson helped pass the 1964 Civil Rights Act banning segregation in public places. The 1965 Voting Rights Act allowed hundreds of thousands of Southern black people to vote for the first time. Civil rights leader Malcolm X felt that the laws did not go far enough and encouraged African Americans to build their own businesses. He was shot in 1965. Martin Luther King, Jr., was killed in 1968. Both leaders inspired advances in civil rights long after their deaths.

Continued Successes

African American "firsts" in politics and other fields have become more numerous.

Lesson 1: Review

1. ⟳ **Cause and Effect** Complete the chart by filling in the effects of these major events of the Civil Rights movement.

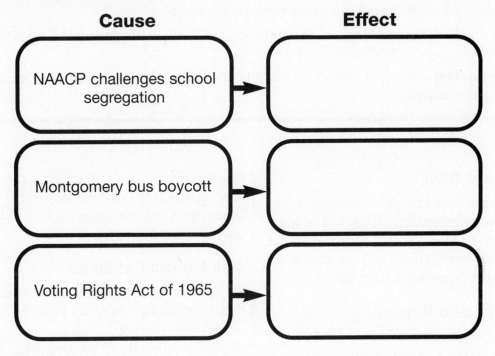

Cause		Effect
NAACP challenges school segregation	→	
Montgomery bus boycott	→	
Voting Rights Act of 1965	→	

2. How did segregation create social isolation?

_____

_____

3. How did Rosa Parks use passive resistance to help change bus segregation laws? Answer in two or more sentences. Use the highlighted terms in your answer.

_____

_____

4. List four events that contributed to the success of the Civil Rights movement.

_____

_____

5. **Critical Thinking:** *Evaluate* What was the importance of the Civil Rights Act of 1964 to all Americans?

_____

_____

© Scott Foresman Growth of a Nation

Lesson 2: The Cold War Continues

Vocabulary

space race the race between countries to explore outer space

Vietnam Conflict the war between communist-backed North Vietnam and U.S.-backed South Vietnam

guerrilla warfare the use of random attacks and other unusual tactics, such as no uniforms and civilians who fight

The Space Race

In 1957 Americans learned the Soviets had launched the first satellite, *Sputnik.* The **space race** began, and the National Aeronautics and Space Administration (NASA) was founded. In 1962 John Glenn orbited the earth.

Apollo 11 and Beyond

In 1969 American astronauts successfully landed on the moon. Today, American and Russian astronauts work together.

Trouble in Southeast Asia

In 1945 communist leader Ho Chi Minh declared Vietnam's independence from France. By 1954, the French wished to withdraw from Vietnam. The Geneva Accords stated that Vietnam should be divided until elections could be held. With support from the Soviet Union and China, Ho Chi Minh fought to unite South Vietnam with communist North Vietnam. Presidents Eisenhower and Kennedy sent money and weapons, as well as soldiers to train the South Vietnamese army. In 1964 President Johnson sent more American soldiers to help South Vietnam fight the communists.

The Vietnam Conflict

By 1968, there were more than 500,000 American soldiers fighting the **Vietnam Conflict.** They were well armed and had air support, but they could not stop the communists, who were very successful with **guerrilla warfare.**

The Conflict at Home

For the first time, people saw a real war on television. Many Americans believed the United States should withdraw from a war that seemed unwinnable. They were called "doves," and they protested the war by marching and staging sit-ins. More radical protesters bombed buildings. "Draft dodgers" burned their draft cards and moved to Canada. People who supported the war were called "hawks." They, too, staged demonstrations. When Richard Nixon was elected President, he thought most Americans supported the war and called them the "silent majority."

The War Ends

In 1973 the United States and North Vietnam signed a cease-fire, and American troops left. In 1975 the South Vietnamese surrendered to the North Vietnamese. Two million Vietnamese and 57,000 Americans had been killed.

Mending Relations

In recent years the United States has worked for better relations with Vietnam, but still wants a full accounting of missing soldiers.

Lesson 2: Review

1. **Summarize** Complete the chart below by summarizing these events.

Events

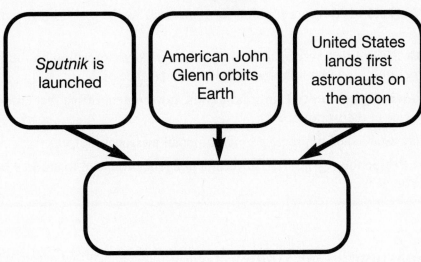

2. What caused the United States to send soldiers to fight in Vietnam?

   _____

   _____

3. How did the Viet Cong's use of guerrilla warfare make the Vietnam Conflict a difficult assignment for American soldiers? Answer in one or more sentences. Use the highlighted terms.

   _____

   _____

4. Describe the different reactions of the doves and hawks to the Vietnam Conflict. Explain why each felt the way they did. Answer in two or more sentences.

   _____

   _____

5. **Critical Thinking: *Point of View*** Was President Johnson a hawk or a dove?

   _____

   _____

Lesson 3: Years of Change

Vocabulary

National Organization for Women an organization for women's rights

United Farm Workers of America a union for improving work conditions for migrant workers

Americans with Disabilities Act an act that prohibits job discrimination on the basis of disability and requires public buildings and services to be accessible

Equal Employment Opportunity Commission the government office that enforces equal opportunity policies in the workplace

Earth Day a day established to promote environmental awareness

Environmental Protection Agency the government agency founded to enforce laws that protect the environment

Unequal Opportunities for Women

Women had the same legal rights as men, but they did not have the same opportunities.

Making Progress

Many people joined the Women's Rights Movement in the 1960s and 1970s. The **National Organization for Women** (NOW) was formed in 1966. The Equal Rights Amendment (ERA), guaranteeing equal treatment of men and women, passed in Congress in 1972. Too few states approved the amendment, so it did not become part of the Constitution. Still, opportunities for women expanded.

Working for Change

Migrant workers moved from farm to farm harvesting crops, working long hours for low pay. In the 1960s and 1970s César Chávez and Dolores Huerta fought for the rights of migrant workers. They formed the **United Farm Workers of America** (UFW). Inspired by the civil rights movement, they used passive resistance to improve working conditions. Also, Native American groups fought to regain rights to land and water. In 1990 the **Americans with Disabilities Act** passed, making it illegal to

refuse to hire a qualified person who has a disability. Public schools must also provide equal access to education.

Opportunities and Recognition

The **Equal Employment Opportunity Commission** was formed in 1965 to enforce civil rights laws in the workplace. It protects people from discrimination on the basis of race or sex. The Civil Liberties Act of 1988 officially apologized to Japanese Americans detained during World War II. In 2001 Navajo veterans of World War II were given Congressional Gold and Silver Medals in recognition for their work as code talkers.

A Cleaner World

After World War II, American conservation efforts improved. In 1962 Rachel Carson wrote *Silent Spring* about the effects of pesticides. In 1970 the first **Earth Day** was held and the **Environmental Protection Agency** was founded.

Looking to the Future

Efforts to protect the environment are working, but people need to stay involved.

© Scott Foresman Growth of a Nation

Lesson 3: Review

1. ↻ **Cause and Effect** Complete the chart below by filling in the effects of these issues during the late 1900s.

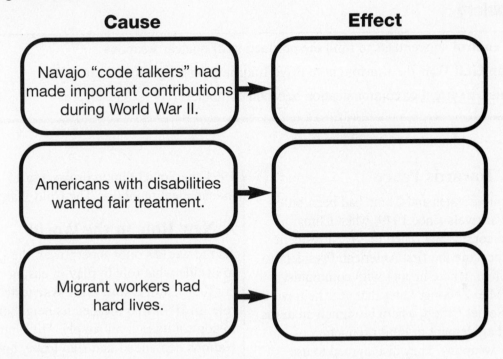

Cause   **Effect**

Navajo "code talkers" had made important contributions during World War II.   →

Americans with disabilities wanted fair treatment.   →

Migrant workers had hard lives.   →

2. How did the Civil Rights movement influence the United Farm Workers of America? Answer in two or more sentences. Use the highlighted term in your answer.

_____

_____

3. What are some difficulties women faced in the mid-1900s? How did the situation change during the 1960s–1980s?

_____

_____

4. What are two ways Americans worked to improve the environment in the late 1900s?

_____

_____

5. **Critical Thinking: *Draw Conclusions*** What conclusion can you draw about your role in the future of the environment? Explain your answer.

_____

_____

Lesson 4: Changing World, Changing Roles

Vocabulary

> **arms control** agreements to limit the production of nuclear weapons
>
> **Persian Gulf War** the war fought to drive Iraqi invaders from Kuwait in 1991
>
> **Internet** a system of communication between computers

Steps Towards Peace

The United States and China had been bitter Cold War rivals since 1949, when China became communist. Then in 1972 President Nixon became the first American President to visit China, where he met with communist leader Mao Zedong. Later that year he traveled to the Soviet Union, where he signed an **arms control** agreement to limit production of nuclear weapons. They also agreed to use space for peaceful purposes. Tensions eased.

Tensions Rise Again

Jimmy Carter was elected President in 1976. He helped Egypt and Israel, longtime enemies, to sign a peace treaty in 1979. The Soviet invasion of Afghanistan in 1979 crushed hopes for lowered Cold War tensions.

The Cold War Ends

In the 1980s, President Ronald Reagan increased spending on weapons and defense. But the Soviet economy was suffering from the arms race. People lacked food and necessities, and they wanted more freedom. Mikhail Gorbachev came into power in 1985 and allowed the Soviet people more political and economic freedom. In 1987 Reagan and Gorbachev signed a new arms control agreement to end the arms race. Some countries in Eastern Europe gained freedom and overthrew their communist governments. The Berlin Wall was destroyed in 1989. In

1991 the Soviet Union broke into 15 independent republics. The Cold War was over.

A New Role in the World

As the world's only superpower, the U.S. had to decide what role to play in easing global conflict. The **Persian Gulf War** tested this role. In 1990 Iraq invaded its neighbor, Kuwait, to control its rich oil supply. The United Nations demanded that Iraq leave, but dictator Saddam Hussein refused. An American-led alliance drove Iraq from Kuwait in 6 weeks. The people of communist Yugoslavia overthrew the government in 1990 and several regions soon declared independence. Violent struggles between ethnic and religious groups broke out. President Clinton sent American soldiers to help restore peace. In 1994 former President Jimmy Carter negotiated a cease-fire. Clinton was impeached in 1998 but not removed from office.

The Internet

The **Internet** was built during the Cold War as a way of communicating in case of a nuclear attack. Today the Internet is used by businesses and individuals, and it has changed the way people communicate.

The End of the Century

In 2000 George W. Bush, son of former President George Bush, defeated Al Gore in one of the closest elections in American history.

Lesson 4: Review

1. 🌀 **Cause and Effect** Complete the chart below by listing three effects of the end of the Cold War.

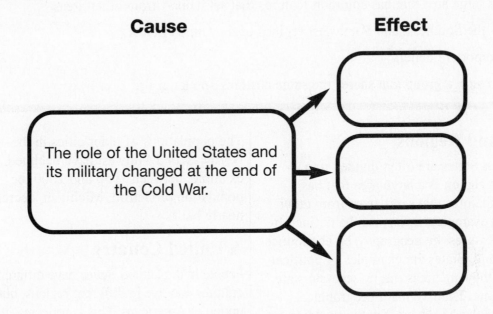

Cause

The role of the United States and its military changed at the end of the Cold War.

Effect

2. How did Nixon's visit to China affect relations between the United States and China?

_____

_____

3. Why did Jimmy Carter invite the leaders of Egypt and Israel to the United States in 1979?

_____

_____

4. How did Mikhail Gorbachev's actions help lead to the collapse of communism in Europe during the 1990s? Answer in two or more sentences. Use the highlighted name in your answer.

_____

_____

5. **Critical Thinking:** *Predict* In what ways do you think the Internet could be used to help people solve conflicts in the future? Answer in one or more sentences. Use the highlighted word in your answer.

_____

_____

Lesson 1: The Fifty States

Vocabulary

region a large area that has common features that set it apart from other areas

Sunbelt the Southeast and Southwest regions of the United States

ideals important beliefs

ethnic group a group that shares the same customs and language

States and Regions

The United States are often divided into regions. A **region** is a large area that has common features that set it apart from other areas. For example, regions can be defined by political features, by geography, by economics, or by culture. States are examples of political regions—they are areas run by separate state governments. The five main geographical regions are the Northeast, Southeast, Midwest, Southwest, and West. Alaska and Hawaii do not border the other states, but they are part of the West.

Americans on the Move

The culture of a region changes when people migrate. Before the mid-1900s, people often lived in one area for their whole lives. Today transportation and communication make it easier for Americans to move. Between 1995 and 2000, nearly half of Americans over age five moved at least once. Often people move to get better jobs. The population of the Southeast and Southwest, the **Sunbelt,** increased after World War II. Many businesses moved to the Sunbelt to take advantage of the warm climate, natural resources, and lower wages. In the early 1900s, many African Americans moved north and west to seek opportunity. Since the Civil Rights Movement, there has been a reverse migration, as many African Americans have moved to the Sunbelt.

The populations of older cities in the Northeast and Midwest have declined. For example, between 1950 and 2000 the population of Detroit, Michigan, decreased by nearly half.

A United Country

People in the United States have different cultures and live in different regions, but are united as Americans. This is reflected in the motto *E Pluribus Unum,* which is Latin for "Out of many, one." This phrase is inscribed in the seal of the United States, as well as on coins and one dollar bills. Americans share basic **ideals,** or important beliefs. These ideals include beliefs about individual freedoms.

A Diverse Country

Part of the rich diversity in the United States comes from its mixture of **ethnic groups.** Until the early 1900s, most immigrants came to the United States from Europe. In the last few decades, most immigrants have come from Asia, Latin America, or Africa. This has increased the number of languages spoken here and the variety of customs and religions. Immigrants often face difficulties and have to learn English. Writer Esmeralda Santiago moved from Puerto Rico to New York City. She found English difficult but learned it and became a successful author.

© Scott Foresman Growth of a Nation

Lesson 1: Review

1. **Summarize** Complete the following chart to summarize the meaning of the motto *E Pluribus Unum*.

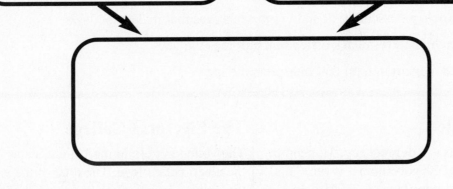

2. Name the five main geographic regions of the United States.

_____

_____

3. Explain why people moved to the Sunbelt after World War II.

_____

_____

4. How has immigration to the United States changed since the late 1900s?

_____

_____

5. **Critical Thinking: *Cause and Effect*** What are some of the effects of immigration to the United States?

_____

_____

Lesson 2: Government of the People

Vocabulary

democracy a country where people have a say in how the government is run

popular sovereignty rule by the people

citizen a member of a country

electoral college the voting system in the United States that says that each state has a number of electors based on its population

Legislative Branch an assembly of state representatives that makes the laws

Executive Branch the President's office that enforces the laws

Judicial Branch a court system that interprets the laws

We the People

The United States is a **democracy.** All people have a say in how the government is run. This idea is also called **popular sovereignty.** In a direct democracy, everyone votes on each decision. However, direct democracy does not work well in large countries like the United States. In a representative democracy, or republic, citizens elect representatives to make laws and run the government for them. The United States is a republic that follows a written plan of government. This makes it a constitutional democracy. The U.S. Constitution was written in 1787.

Citizens at Work

A **citizen** is a member of the country with certain rights and responsibilities. The Constitution protects the rights of citizens, including freedom of speech, freedom of religion, and the right to a fair trial. All citizens over 18 have the right and responsibility to vote. Citizens have the responsibility to obey the law. Adults must also serve on juries and pay taxes to help the government pay for services such as education, protection, and roads and bridges. Citizens can call or write political leaders to express their opinions in peaceful ways.

The Electoral College

The voting system in the United States is called the **electoral college.** The total of the votes by the citizens is called the popular vote. Citizens' votes in each state count toward a number of electors. The number of electors for each state is the same as the number of representatives the state has in Congress. This protects states with smaller populations. The candidate who wins the popular vote in a state gets all of the state's electoral votes. In the 2000 presidential election, Al Gore won the popular vote. But George W. Bush took the majority of the votes in the electoral college and became President.

The Living Constitution

The Constitution is called a "living document" because it can be changed with the addition of amendments. The Constitution set up three branches of government. The **Legislative Branch,** led by Congress, makes the laws. The **Executive Branch,** led by the President, enforces the laws. The **Judicial Branch,** or the court system, interprets the laws. All three branches meet in Washington, D.C. The highest court in the United States, the Supreme Court, determines if laws follow the Constitution. The President appoints Supreme Court judges, who must then be approved by the Senate.

© Scott Foresman Growth of a Nation

Lesson 2: Review

1. ⟳ **Summarize** Complete this chart by filling in the details for the summary about the United States government.

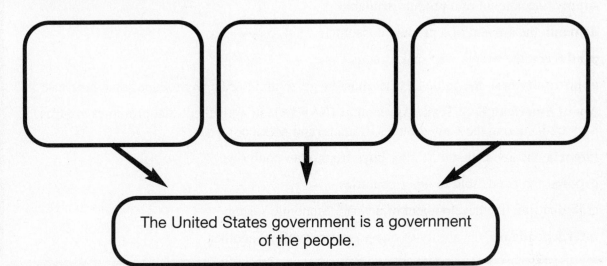

The United States government is a government of the people.

2. List some of the rights and responsibilities of United States citizenship.

_____

_____

3. How is the winner of a presidential election determined?

_____

_____

4. **Critical Thinking:** *Decision Making* Do you think the electoral college system is an effective way to choose the President? Why or why not?

_____

_____

5. What makes the constitution a "living document"?

_____

_____

Lesson 3: Economy and Trade

Vocabulary

supply the amount of a product available

demand the amount of a product consumers want to buy

producers the people who make goods

opportunity cost the value of what must be given up in order to produce something else

North American Free Trade Agreement (NAFTA) an agreement that promotes tax-free trade among the United States, Canada, and Mexico

imports the goods that a country buys from other countries

exports the goods sold to other countries

globalization the development of a world economic system

interdependence the ability of one economy to affect another

Supply and Demand

The system of **supply** and **demand** determines prices in a free enterprise system. **Producers** can set a high price for an item if there is high demand from consumers. Limited supply also drives prices up. Low demand and large supply drive prices down. Businesses must also consider the **opportunity cost** of making something.

Twenty-first Century Jobs

The future's jobs may be different than today's. Computers changed the job market in the 1990s. Most jobs today involve computer skills. People are living longer and enjoying second and third careers. The health care field is growing to help older Americans live healthier lives. The fastest-growing career not related to computers is in home health care.

Technology and Life

Computers have changed how we work, learn, play, and communicate. By 2001 more than half the people in the country were using the Internet, and more than 90 percent of students ages 5 to 17 use computers. Satellite technology supports cellular phones, pagers, cable television, wireless Internet service, and Global Positioning Systems in cars.

International Trade

Technology and international trade connect the economies of different countries. In 1992 the **North American Free Trade Agreement** (NAFTA) was signed to encourage trade among the United States, Canada, and Mexico. The three countries do not tax each other's **imports** and **exports.**

Globalization

Globalization has resulted in people and goods flowing freely between countries and **interdependence.** It has also affected culture, since people all over the world can see the same movies, hear the same music, and even buy the same clothes.

Technology and Change

Just one person can develop new technology and change society, such as An Wang, working with computers in the 1950s.

© Scott Foresman Growth of a Nation

Lesson 3: Review

1. ⟳ **Cause and Effect** Complete this chart by filling in the effect that you could expect based on the rule of supply and demand.

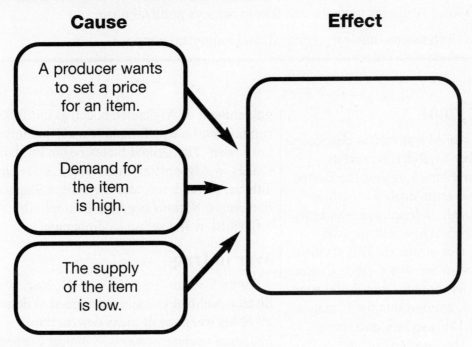

Cause

A producer wants to set a price for an item.

Demand for the item is high.

The supply of the item is low.

Effect

2. What job fields are expected to grow the most during the early 2000s?

_____

_____

3. How does technology affect the way Americans live and work?

_____

_____

4. How has the United States government's policy on trade changed?

_____

_____

5. **Critical Thinking:** *Draw Conclusions* Globalization and international trade have created worldwide interdependence. Consider the advantages and disadvantages of this, then write whether or not you think this is a positive trend and why.

_____

_____

Lesson 1: New Dangers

Vocabulary

terrorist an individual who uses violence and fear to achieve political goals

weapons of mass destruction nuclear, chemical, and biological weapons

September 11, 2001

Sometimes the course of history can change in a day. On September 11, 2001, **terrorists** carried out a massive attack against the United States. Terrorists are individuals who achieve political goals through violence and fear. Early in the morning terrorists hijacked, or used force to take over, four airplanes. Two crashed into the twin towers of the World Trade Center in New York City, where more than 2,800 were killed. A third plane crashed into the Pentagon, the Department of Defense headquarters in Washington, D.C. The fourth plane, where it seems the passengers tried to retake control of the plane, crashed into a field in Pennsylvania. More than 3,000 people died in the attacks. There were victims from 90 different countries.

Americans United

New York City firefighters and police officers rushed into the burning buildings of the World Trade Center and were killed when the buildings collapsed. Americans united in support of the victims, donating blood, food, and money. New York Mayor Rudolf Giuliani and President Bush praised Americans for their courage and generosity in response to the attacks.

The Struggle Against Terrorism

The United States determined that the attacks were planned by the Al Qaeda terrorist group, led by Osama bin Laden, originally from Saudi Arabia. Al Qaeda was based in Afghanistan and opposed American influence in the Middle East. It had carried out several attacks against U.S. embassies and ships in the past. The United States demanded that the government of Afghanistan, called the Taliban, capture bin Laden. Taliban leaders supported bin Laden. The United States began military strikes in Afghanistan in October, 2001. The Taliban surrendered, and the United States and the United Nations began to help rebuild Afghanistan and set up a democracy.

War in Iraq

After the Persian Gulf War in 1991, Iraqi dictator Saddam Hussein had agreed to destroy all of his **weapons of mass destruction,** including nuclear weapons, chemical weapons, and weapons that spread disease. Over the next 12 years, Hussein did not cooperate with U.N. weapons inspectors. Condoleeza Rice, the U.S. National Security Advisor, believed that Hussein would be a serious threat if he were hiding weapons of mass destruction. In March 2003, the Bush administration decided to use military force to remove Hussein from power. Leaders of many countries did not believe war was justified and wanted to allow the United Nations to continue inspections. Thirty countries supported the American and British troops, who quickly defeated the Iraqi army. The process of rebuilding began.

Rebuilding at Home

The Pentagon was repaired within a year of the attacks. Workers at the World Trade Center removed 100,000 truckloads of debris. Designs for new buildings were part of the plan for rebuilding the World Trade Center site. In response to the attacks, the government started the new Department of Homeland Security in 2003.

Lesson 1: Review

1. 🔄 **Summarize** Complete this chart by filling in the most important details from this lesson and then fill in a summary of the details.

Terrorists attacked the United States on September 11, 2001.

2. Summarize the terrorist attacks of September 11, 2001.

_____

_____

3. In what ways did Americans unite in response to the attacks?

_____

_____

4. What military actions did the United States take after September 11, 2001?

_____

_____

5. **Critical Thinking:** *Analyze Primary Sources* You read that New York City Mayor Rudolph Giuliani said of the September 11 attack: "This terrorist attack was intended to break our spirit. It has utterly failed." What evidence could be used to support this statement?

_____

_____

Lesson 2: Looking Ahead

Vocabulary

atmosphere the gases that surround a planet

global warming the theory that Earth is slowly warming due to an increase in carbon dioxide

artificial intelligence a machine with the ability to learn and imitate human thought

Protecting the Environment

One challenge in the future is to find ways to produce energy that does not harm the environment. Burning gasoline and coal creates carbon dioxide, and scientists believe that increased carbon dioxide in the earth's **atmosphere** is causing the climate to slowly become warmer. **Global warming** would cause environmental problems around the world. New energy sources are needed. For example, hydrogen-powered cars use a source of energy that does not pollute the air.

Global Solutions

Global challenges include fighting disease, hunger, war, lack of freedom, and extreme poverty. Today there are 1 billion people in the world living on less than one dollar a day. Malaria and AIDS are causing millions of deaths in Africa. The United Nations has made a list of "Development Goals" that the world hopes to achieve by 2015. Former U.S. President Jimmy Carter is one of many people working to make these goals a reality. He was awarded the 2002 Nobel Peace Prize for his work fighting disease and supporting free elections around the world.

Looking Forward

Scientist Michio Kaku thinks the next 100 years will "witness an even more far-reaching scientific revolution" than that of the past 100 years. For example, scientists are working on a computer chip that may help people with brain damage. Others are working to build machines with **artificial intelligence,** or the ability to learn and imitate human thought. Also, NASA is working on vehicles that it plans to use to explore Mars. Many changes are anticipated. Do you have your own ideas about life in the future? For example, what do you think will be the most important invention of this century? Will new medicines allow most people to live more than 100 years? Will we find new ways to conserve resources and protect our environment? Do you think we will succeed in ending terrorism and stopping war? In the future, you and your classmates will be the ones who will help answer these questions.

Lesson 2: Review

1. **Main Idea and Details** Complete this chart by filling in details that support the main idea shown below.

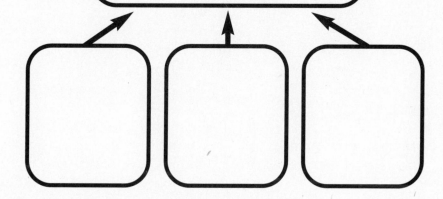

Individuals, organizations, and countries are working to solve global problems and improve life in the future.

2. If hydrogen cars become practical, how could they help prevent global warming?

   _____

   _____

3. Describe three global problems that people are working to solve.

   _____

   _____

4. What are three projects that scientists are working on today?

   _____

   _____

5. **Critical Thinking: *Predict*** Reread the list of questions at the end of the previous page. Pick one of these questions, or write a question of your own about the future. Then write a one-page essay in which you answer this question with your own predictions about the future.

   _____

   _____

NOTES